PARKS AND RECREATION

Life Writing

ABIGAIL GEORGE

Edited by Tendai Rinos Mwanaka

Mwanaka Media and Publishing Pvt Ltd,
Chitungwiza Zimbabwe
*
Creativity, Wisdom and Beauty

Publisher: Mmap
Mwanaka Media and Publishing Pvt Ltd
24 Svosve Road, Zengeza 1
Chitungwiza Zimbabwe
mwanaka@yahoo.com
www.africanbookscollective.com/publishers/mwanaka-media-and-publishing
https://facebook.com/MwanakaMediaAndPublishing/

Distributed in and outside N. America by African Books Collective
orders@africanbookscollective.com
www.africanbookscollective.com

ISBN: 978-1-77929-611-5
EAN: 9781779296115

DISCLAIMER
All views expressed in this publication are those of the author and do not
necessarily reflect the views of *Mmap*.

Dedication

For mummy and daddy, with love!
For Virgil Bruiners, a trusted shield!

Table of Contents

Endorsements

Parks and Recreation

"A Bessie Head-reincarnate, Abigail George is an architect of satire, visual imagery and verbal dexterity. *Parks and Recreation* is a confessional but a paradoxical revelation punctuated by stream of consciousness and an author's defiance to the traditional obviousity and patriarchal barbarism or tendencies. The author mirrors her state of being, her personality and societal odds with unwarranted boldness. She demystifies traditional social norms as vagaries with the defiance of a wounded tiger. Her stories scatter away barbaric patriarchal customs with the sharpness of moonlight light arrows to the shadows of darkness. Bessie Head's writing bones have risen in writer, poet and agent of change Abigail George."

Mbizo Chirasha (Zimbabwe)
PEN Deutschland Recipient of Exiled Writer Grant 2017

Parks and Recreation is a collection of short stories which skilfully evokes graphic pictures of human life with the help of apt images and symbols derived from the everyday life. It presents an account of different subjects that one witnesses and faces in this world – it has all: the echoes, calls and the cry of world – but more important an intellectual will – extraordinary presentation with an uncoiling spring of human foreboding and inevitability – narrating the stories of unforgettable characters. Stories are well paced and evocative. It is, indeed, a masterpiece written in a simple and unpretentious language.

Dr. Rajeshwar Prasad (India)
Associate Professor and Head of the English Department

"Abigail George's *Parks and Recreation* is a literary feast of beautiful stories that throb with heartache, loss and love. The stories are told with the grace of prose poetry and are grounded in the complex lives of the characters that populate the book. It is a comforting book, I know of no reader that this lovely collection of stories will not speak to. I heartily recommend this lovely book of stories of the heart."

Ikhide R. Ikheloa (USA)
Literary critic

Abigail George's words are rich, and sublimely textured, much like a precious, well-loved handmade patchwork quilt. One sinks almost immediately into the familiarity, warmth and comfort of her detailed and delicate prose. Her writing flows fluidly and is almost unbearably evocative. Her stories, while embracing universal themes of love, loss, change and choices, are all unique but seem to be interwoven with one another. Layers of lush words wash over all one's senses with her detailed descriptions of times, places, feelings and characters. Visceral and vivid, no part of one's awareness is left untouched or unaffected. Abigail George is a formidable story teller and this book will shock, move and inspire.

Desiree-Anne Martin (South Africa)
Author of *We Don't Talk About It. Ever.*

Abigail George is an explosive writer from South Africa who in her stories makes every word count due to her encapsulating in them her powerful emotions. The narrator in every story almost is first person and a woman and thus one guesses at a substratum of autobiography or personal experience in the stories, but rising above that is her real gift, which is about taking the reader on a journey into the depths of the human psyche and of a life in South Africa, its complexities and vicissitudes, its pain and struggle and its isolated triumphs. The history of the place and its burdens and the poetry of the place is etched poignantly in story after story. Hers is writing that has to be cherished and made known to the world, writing from the heart and body and gut, that leaves one richly repaid for having read it. My only advice to people thus is to read and enjoy her work which is worth it, as in it flickers the fires of all good writing, its bone and marrow, its joints and sinews.

Dr Ampat Koshy (Kingdom of Saudi Arabia)
Assistant professor and award-winning author

Smile Daddy Please!

I was born into the wild of this country. A wilderness of steel wasteland; sky and street shadow me like the white sun, yellow moon, star Hiroshima, moon Nagasaki people, thumbprints trapped on pages of long overdue library books. There are incidents that cannot be accounted for and the world is still, even when coming home from the sea. The sand is like diamonds in my shoes and my hair. There's already a set rhythm, a resurrection of a child to a woman; a drowning woman in half-life, a wild flailing thing. Bloodlines are visible from the neck down in peacock-blue circles, which slip beneath the surface, like threads no one can see. There was another woman in the house, my doppelganger. Grief burned her in a rush of women-speak. So, as cat wrestles with bird, a mess of feathers everywhere and as red dots appear, I feel light-headed like I could disappear into thin air, with the mercy of flight because you, the sane me is no longer here.

So, what if I know these playing fields like the back of my hand; these frontiers and borders of my own childhood making. I wish you were here daddy. Darkness comes to me even when I am lying in a hospital bed but I'm not bitter, just tired. I'm past that stage. When that wave comes there's a thrill. They have a name for it. They're calling it clinical depression. I am the one who has to live with it. I am 'the experiment', the case study under observation who cannot sleep in the dark. There's a mirror above the sink in my room and bars at the window. I don't think 'they' (the establishment) wants us to think that we're prisoners though. They want us to be safe, to feel as if we are well looked after. My mother can't even look at me when she comes to visit with my dad.

They make excuses for the others, the rest of the family, the cousins I never see anyway, the aunts and uncles that seemed to have vanished into the thin blue air, my brother and my sister. They harp on that they're tired, they're studying toward their examinations and then (it took me years) before I realized they were on their own emotional journey and I was on mine. And if three different individual's journeys weren't destined to meet then I had to make peace with that. But somehow, they forgot that I bleed as they do. I'm human. Doesn't everyone bleed? Everything tastes metallic here even the texture of the sandwiches we get served at tea and before we go to bed. The Milo makes me gag but I drink it anyway. It's warm and milky. It fills me up. There's a routine here like the military. I have grown accustomed to the nurses outfitted in their navy. They move like ghosts.

But the thing is the in-patients move around the building and the rooms in exactly the same way. Here in the hospital reality is blurred into a mix of auditory and visual hallucinatory images and sometimes there's something schizophrenic about mealtimes, the scrambled eggs, fish fingers on your plate, the voices coming from the next bed or room during visiting hours. Yet it gives me a sense of comfort to know I am surrounded by the nurses' physical health, their emotional wellbeing that I am certain they take for granted for, with their soothing choirgirl-choirboy voices, neat little haircuts and flashy, toothy ad-perfect and mint-fresh grins. You get to do a lot of imagining and resting when you're four to a room in high care. You have all the time in the world to sketch in compositions, write notes to yourself, and have whole conversations with yourself about the girl who left in the middle of the night with an ambulance. She wore black all the time, even black nail polish and told you to watch out for her, that she was a Goth and could invoke a higher power.

Then there was the woman who woke you up in the middle of the night and told you that she was the reincarnation of Jesus. She wanted to read Scriptures to you, quote it at you. But it was the middle of the night and you weren't resting anymore and you didn't want to imagine the end of the world at midnight, so you told her she could tell you in the morning what the future was going to be like. You were sleepy, your head like wool, just about to fall asleep so you told her before you turned around to go back to bed. You weren't being brave just nonplussed. There were days when courage failed me and when I had no voice to speak of or opinion. There were just the chemicals interacting in my bloodstream nourishing me, feeding, overwhelming and hospitalized me. All my stamina was leaking out of me and I was left apathetic. I didn't want to eat with the other people. It was a pretty room with cheerful curtains at the window, wooden tables and chairs. It was supposed to feel homey.

But I found sanctuary in my bed, the white linen with the word 'hospital' written in blue, bold letters with thread, with me feeling blue as well but not so bold as all that. I could feel the sky as I walked outside. It was a sensation that I thought an addict would probably feel. I remember my flight from Johannesburg as if it was yesterday and the impulse of the recollection of the powerful flow and energy of the haze that came with it. I remembered feeling that all sense had left me and all I was left with was intuition. This was wrong and that was right. Red signaled danger to me as if something not of this world, alien and subversive was trying to contact me. There weren't voices in my head but everything was heightened. My insomnia and confusion and when and if I were confused the world around me was a television world.

And there I was the camera, seeing, viewing everything around me as if it was a kaleidoscope or a foreign film with subtitles in a language I couldn't understand. Noise was louder. Traffic was a line of cars blocking my way through to get back home to my parents. All I wanted was the two of them looking at me with pride and love, loving me in the state I was in and addressing it. I knew by instinct that they would know what to do. I wanted peace. I wanted quiet. I told the cab driver to turn his radio down and I refused to pay him. I said that I had no money. But he was determined in his own way. He said that I had to pay him. So, I told him to wait and knocked on my front door. Everyone was still sleeping. No one knew I had come home. No one knew that anything was wrong yet. I still had the ghost of a blue shirt and cigarettes and the language of first love inside my heart, parading around my head as if I had given it permission to be there.

Of course, when they took one hard and long look at me they knew something was wrong. Was it drugs? No, it wasn't drugs. I had to say that with commitment. My mother gave me money to pay for the cab. In the days that followed I wrote on walls (my own brand of graffiti), I drew pictures in my own blood. I pasted broken glass on cardboard and called it 'art', flipped out when I was confronted and colored as if I was in school for beginners again, calling the faces in a rainbow of watercolors 'my angels'. I would take a knife when everyone in the house had gone to bed, the one with the sharpest edge in the kitchen drawer and just to take 'the heat off of things' I would 'cut' myself (though not very deep). Just enough to wound my spirit, to remind myself I was alive, part of the living, a human being. My parents were nice about it in a sane way. They would tell me how sick I was making myself.

I had to stop doing that (they didn't like the pictures I was drawing), that I was still their child, their daughter and that they loved me. I wished they had said that over and over again. I wish I could remember them saying that they loved me over and over again but my mother began to see past the things that I was doing and on the whole my father ignored me. He had his own depression and his own questions. For my mother it was obvious that all the turn of events in the household since I returned from Johannesburg was psychological in origin. So, the role she had played in my father's life since they were married was one she had to repeat with me. I don't know who brought up the discussion of 'going to see the psychiatrist' first. I can't remember very well how I got there only that I was in a hospital. There was a passage with lots of white doors and names of doctors on them.

Receptionists sat with ledgers in front of them writing down the name of the next appointment, and soon this scrawny, lovely young woman though one with her hair bobbing around her face would write down my name and the date for my next appointment. Soon I came to one of those doors and it was my mother who opened the door. I can't remember if the door was already open but I do know this. She was the one who was holding my hand, leading me in, into my future and not my father. It has taken me over a decade to confess this and no one thing, unfortunate event, a death in the family has led up to it. She's gone, gone, gone, a lot of people who knew the private and the public persona of me could have said. I didn't listen to anyone's negativity but my own. People stopped talking to me. It was then that I decided on the doppelganger, the two me's, the blue, depressed me with the sorrowful face and the intense writer of 'into the black divide' poetry.

Then there was the other me, the manic interloper intertwined with that most intense part of me together like yin and yang. The one couldn't exist without the other. I was all of nineteen with youth being 'the grass is always greener' side on the one hand and on the other side darkness was always visible. And at some point, food in all of this, the 'wasted decade', all that time I had lost became my friend, the best friend with the sweet face I never had. Food would smile at me all the time, love me when I was up or down, reward me when I was anxious or raging, furious at myself most of all because all I had to do was to take a pill. There was one for sleeping, one to stabilize the mood and then there was one for the depression. Other people's lot in life was hell and compared to theirs mine was a corner of paradise. Before I became ill, diagnosed and really started to suffer I liked eating cake and then I started loving it up too much.

5

Stuffing the cream and the butter icing in my mouth and licking my lips. Broccoli was boring and vegetables too nutritious. I slowly started to hate the mirror, that most perfect looking glass. If the eyes are the windows to the soul, I soon felt that I could never meet that gaze that was once so fiercely independent of other people around her again. I had failed so many people, my grandmother, my mother and my sister, modern society. I had wounded myself with serious intent. Lesser, although I don't like to think of any person in this human race as being lesser, mortals have been punished for that. I still do not like to think of what women my age are doing. The wild, single life or the quiet home life of newlywed bliss.

Those who are of the marrying kind and who celebrate their birthdays with their friends eating restaurant suppers in seafood restaurants. I am not that kind of woman. I left that power-driven, power-hungry world behind me. It didn't embrace me anyway. I know what other people think of me and the way I live in. It doesn't fit in with society's norms and values. I do not value the material things of this life.

I sense more the spiritual basis and home of things. I hold that dear. I hold onto it for life. It moves me in this golden aftermath, graces the internal, what I feel is most pure. It is what I hope to glide on from this world to the one in the hereafter.

When Bad Mothers Happen

Keeping secrets is stupid. It's going to come out anyway.

'Money cometh. Money cometh. Money cometh.' My mother would sing throughout the house as she scribbled on her Lotto paper, willing the winning numbers to come to her from the universe.

'Speak in tongues throughout the house. Pray. Don't look at me with those big eyes of yours.'

My sister worships her. Whenever they talk on the phone, I feel a stab, a killing.

These days I find myself envying pregnant women, that belly filled with life, a heart beating away. Married career women, beautiful women, pretty teenagers who are vain and daring but secretly despise making themselves heard, having a voice and who are less than hard working. They never have to work at saying, 'Look at me. I am hungry for life, learning and love.' Instead, my family finds my work wholly uninspiring. You suffer when you hold on to the fight for your voice to be heard.

'Say the *Our Father* instead of smoking.' My mother had a habit of saying. I cannot unlock her heart. It is vanishing in front of my eyes. It's as plain as day. A secret in a Pandora's Box of them.

The silence in this house has shaped me. Its sword, every place found inside out of darkness, even bone, the kitchen table, my family. Now I know what summer is for. Not just for time spent on the beach or potato salad melting in salad cream whipped into a bowl, for swimming or ice clinking in the glass. It's for escape.

'Don't stand in my light.'

As a learner I was drawn to poets, their spiritual existence so perhaps my literary efforts reflect that.

'Get out, you. I'm sleeping.'

I'm too upset even to think. It burns me to think of everything I could have. I couldn't get up this morning.

'Take your Smarties yet.'

I have nothing to give you. I don't know how to treat men delicately. Maybe it has something to do with my mother, hearing her voice and when she doesn't speak I can still hear her in my head. Maybe I should work harder at seeing her point-of-view instead of pouting and eating seconds so much.

Skinny-Legs-Spaghetti talks too much. She minds everybody's business and listens at doors. I hate Skinny-Legs-Spaghetti. I don't want her to talk to me anymore. Nobody understands why I am depressive least of all me. Every secret chance I get I live on the edge vicariously through other people who assume wrong impressions like the aesthetic mishap that an artist painted on the canvas of his subject like that of the narcissist Dorian Grey. The drowned, disowned; those who inherited a fate like tortured public perverts and those that fade away. Their black hearts and dark minds and black tongues, their weak and panic-stricken hearts racing. Money is their aphrodisiac, their dirty mouths filled with secrets and lies, they live at high speed, electric and in sunlight they can even be angelic and night time their beauty is on fire.

I loved the 'Superman' movies. I'm a Superwoman on a high of some kind of wonderful day ahead. On days like this the water curls around my body like a blue bubble. Here I am not a mistake, I do not need an introduction, I am not a shell of a girl child, I don't have to be popular or a rich girl. I am buoyant in this oblivion. I can heal everyone as I taught myself to do and teach people to be unafraid. I shiver, tangled in a web of causes. The wind is like a paper cut but a hopeful optimism is like a fever inside of me crawling from the pit of my stomach. There are no ripples on

8

the surface, bursts and showers; truths spilling forth from the mouths of babes, silly, nosy kids or soul mates – likeminded rogues, extremists and sensualists you'll never meet. I am not an insomniac. Here I sleep to dream. My lips are wet.

No one knows the meaning of this life – life and death – more than the hobo curled up sleeping in a heap at the mosque. We are doing field research for my father for the next book he is writing. I am happy to be an interloper learning about my father's past, our country's painful history, the sorrow that yielded the strange, unforgiving stillness here by this fig tree that I am so touched by. The hateful images of these injustices of Apartheid and the Group Areas Act stay long after. From here you can see the harbour, fishing boats bopping up and down on the choppy waves still untouched in another passage in eternity.

The inner city has become an underground sin city, a ghost world, neon glowing urban and a wasteland wilderness. Pimps and drug-dealers, handsome, well-heeled, well-dressed, talk to a buyer on their cell phone. They are masters of disguise, vanishing acts, disappearing into thin air.

Thin prostitutes, prostitutes with slippery, shiny hair that falls down their back, curly, blonde, dyed, who don wigs, with beautiful, shiny, healthy afros, with their thigh-high leather scuffed boots that skim their miniskirts or jeans, wasted or high, or pregnant, their foreheads invisible by a dark-haired, blonde, blunt fringe – their lives are for rent. They do not smile or laugh; they draw invisible motifs of pretty and red tattoos on their skin with a needle or a chipped and dirty fingernail. They toss their hair back from their faces made-up with dirty make-up, their lies, vulnerability, tenderness is transparent and their shoulder blades are cool.

The criminal world of the drug dealers, some of whom were immigrants, revealed to me that they had a celebrated affliction to harm not out of spite but out of a backward, awkward survival mechanism. They were self-styled nomads, hunters, warriors, gatherers and dreamers, survivors and freedom fighters trapped, trying against all odds to flee entrapment with a mechanical urgency, with the wisdom of awesome and powerful beasts. The way they viewed the world was not fresh and clean. Like the food they ate was neither a feast, nor did it sate their appetite. The money that came to them, the more problems they saw.

There is a lifetime of ambition there if a prostitute uses her mind at the devotion of her soul. They are artistic, sadistic voyeurs, fragile, their all-consuming greed, hunger attractive and yet, unspeakable. Their lifestyle is forbidden yet it is still permissive. It is frozen in time from the golden and ancient days of mistresses and courtesans. In the walls of the rooms of their love, I imagine, as our car speeds past the cheap, dingy hotels, love is not giving. It is a painful pill to swallow, their breath is like a sweet but unwholesome mist, and their vision distorted and burns a host of disturbing and troublesome portrayals of people on their brains that does not give any psychological relief.

If the evening or the tawdry affair has been a disaster there will be more hell to pay with more violence if there is not any money.

They are in this world but not of it. For the ladies of the night, it is midnight all day for them and all night.

This is how my city, my hometown Port Elizabeth is at night.

Underwater everything is distilled, cleansed and purified. Demonstrating the cool rebirth of your soul, leaving you coming up for air, shaking, trembling, breathless and warning you not to swallow more than a mouthful.

The cracks become gold flecked. Even as your lungs start to feel as if they could burst, you stay at the bottom of the pool, an ice queen frozen in time, a cold, ungenerous, unfeeling thing and an innocent. Deserts can bloom, even human ones but it is only red flowers that can bloom at the bottom of this swimming pool.

A swimming pool is like air. A temporary exercise in therapy, breathing lessons in survival, relevant and dangerous. Everything that is trapped in a

10

box, that hums, which buzzes like bees inside my brain, like the drops of dewy water, cling to my hair and my fingertip, as sound and tension escapes.

The kick, the telepathic life and birth of the first indescribable tug of a high reverses a lifetime of bad habits, self-destruction, makes your sad childhood seem breezy, it transforms the negative into the positive, the world is insatiable and you have to have all of it, be nourished by all of it before it destroys you and you come down. It is downhill from there afterwards as you search for your next fix.

The first kick as I pull away from the wall, the telepathic life, birth of every stroke, everything that sparked my reverie disappears. I am no longer infatuated with the black mood as it lifts. Each stranglehold no longer wipes me out. There is nobody here at the swimming pool to see me reaching for life that takes each breath away and gives me one back completing me. I am still in the land of the living and the world in which everything wrong seems dangerously right. It is almost as if it has become a nuisance to say that Africa is not normal. Normal is a very seductive word. It does not give you nightmares.

I imagine that food is too exotic to eat. I read somewhere that you do not eat when you are on a drug-induced high. It is like taking an appetite suppressant. I suppose that is why the modelling business went through a phase termed 'heroine-chic'. Why pretty premature girls stuck needles into their arms, made themselves sick, did not eat and died from being malnourished.

Women who are not physically and emotionally there for them always inconvenience men. Especially alpha males with their fast cars, their degrees, their power trips. I can really see that it is not about love for them. We are all conditioned or socialised from the time that we are very young to be accepted.

I surrender delicate like scent to the light and to the sun's rays. My lashes are wet. It is the end of the world for me. It is a new day. This feeling that I feel is a radical one.

I was running on my own personal velocity with a rock, paper and scissors in my hand and didn't even know it. Often, I would wonder about other people's children. How they lived, what would make the corners of their mouths rise up into a smile or laughter, what their mothers and fathers were like, did they have emptiness and fear rushing through them, suggesting their every move and role in society. Did they play at mud pies, cowboys and crooks, tea parties and dolls and families like Ivy League scientists? Before I entered youth, I wanted to be adventurous. When I did, I was timid. Fear was my constant companion. I would never laugh like the class clown or the other children. I would pretend my childhood was shot in colour. I would click frame by frame into photograph-heaven. By the time I reached youth, I had different pictures of children. All plays of innocence shot in colour inside my head.

They would tick alongside the sound of imagination, its roar hidden in the beautiful and symmetry. Rain hitting the pavement, branches hitting a window in the middle of the night like someone, people trying to get into the house, song, the wind, a choir, music. Words being recited out loud as if a child was reading out loud from a book, an actor from a script. Youth and adulthood for me were childhood continued. I would dream in a filmmaker's dream shot list. There were shots in my dream of Port Elizabeth but it wouldn't be any kind of Port Elizabeth that I knew. It would be grainy, blurred, out of focus, disjointed. It would leave me feeling displaced and my features contorted by rage or a sense of futility. All that remained of Port Elizabeth was spaghetti thin me with my skinny legs walking into a city skyline at night, walking onto a luxurious ocean liner, a big, beautiful boat.

Surrounded by a crowd of extras, no an army of them really, who would vanish from my sight as the daylight filtered through the curtains in my bedroom. What is normal? Normal I discovered was to be the opposite of everything I said and represented, put forward in this world as truth and even my anger, when it spun out of control into rage or petered out, dissolved into the thin blue air. I was always open to suggestions.

I cared for them with my whole heart to tell you the truth. My mother would either scream or shout them at me (always at me) with a heavy streak of venom and aggression in her voice. It would rise like the stars, the boots of pale soldiers marching to their doom until I couldn't see or think straight. I could never wish that negative energy away that I heard inside her voice.

It made me feel that feeling (you know the one you get when you're stuck in a situation, numb, terrified to the bone, a desolate wave washing over you, the shame of humiliation). I always got that feeling whenever I saw a swastika, Hitler, images from a concentration camp, survivors of a concentration camp being interviewed. I would feel desolate, a shrinking violet, a painted wallflower, cold, always cold, as if I was made up of a frozen wasteland and that was my lot in life and I would just have to accept it. And I have always wondered if she despised some part of me, and which part was it. The part that reminded her that I was like her or that I was different from her. It was always the sounds of imagination that would rescue me or more to the point its season (always summer sun), its feast (the roast on Sundays) and its pathways that would lead to a fork in the road.

It's an enchanting feeling detaching yourself from the physical and feeling a giddy sense of displacement from what is real, chemical, skeleton and what is illusion. It is like watching an ant switched on with the magic of all their specific rituals through a magnifying glass as if a voyeur is watching it. Detaching 'you' from the personal velocity of places, things, buildings, marching people, engaging scenarios running on empty or the rush of familiarity. She would hiss like a snake with her snake eyes, the curve of the snake in her hips and her spine or hiss at me like someone who had a lisp.

'Get that devil out of your mouth. I command the spirit of smoking to leave you now. We don't want it. We don't need it. Go. Go. Go. Go now.'

'I'm going to smack you if you don't quit that now. I'll be over there in a second. Watch it, woman.'

If only the two of them, my brother and mother could read these words, hear how absurd they sounded. That's just how we are. Loud, rough, boisterous, tough on the outside, made of jelly on the inside.

My father puts on his apron. He is going to wash the dishes. I close the bathroom door and hear the key clink in the door. Peace (alone?) at last. I am going to run a bath. I open the hot water tap and make lots of bubbles to cheer me up.

There are various ways to become a slave. One of them is becoming a child again, being bossed around by an authority figure, usually a parent. But there's only one way to feel alone. We all feel lonely at some point in our lives. We come into this world armed with nothing and leave it the same way we came. Building walls around you and then usually the walls turned into a fence and left you wondering how you got here, how did 'that' get here complete with electrical wiring to keep everyone out, at a neat distance.

I'll tell you a secret. Inside my head I have a picture of a child's shoes, a child putting them on, tying the laces, reaching out for a parent's hand. I call it 'The Perfect Childhood'. It's a winning formula because it shows the perfect combination of emotional stability (sanity, darling) and an engaged parent. The other picture is one of my intense, goddess-like mother and she's baking. She's in the kitchen and she smells like freshly baked cookies

14

and creamy goodness. I'm just a kid pouting, hoping she'll let me lick the spoon and the bowl out. She is washing her hands under running water in the sink and takes off her ring and puts it, as an afterthought, on the kitchen windowsill. She has dough on her wedding ring. My father will have to take it in again and the last time we went they didn't want to take it. I pout. Oh, I am becoming so good at this.

I've never felt this sense of peace before. I've let go of the materialism of this (what has been years now, more than a decade and a half) wicked, cruel world, unpacked all the sadness. The anger has fizzled out of me. All gone, gone, and gone. Nothing's left, there's nothing left to embrace of that fine, magnificent girl child. She stands, sits, poses in photographs with her chin up in spite of the emotional scarring that came with childhood, that came with an elegant, modern-thinking mother designed by motherhood, that numbing, dense forest of shade, black and white, silhouetted against a pale, grey sky kind of loneliness. That girl who told herself over and over not to fall apart, not to cry, become emotional, that she was not as sensitive as everyone around her made her out to be, I must be loved, no, worshipped, even better, adored. I close my eyes. I just don't want to think anymore.

It hurts to think and that space between dream and reality seems to inch closer to each other until it becomes blurred and leaves me teary-eyed, sobbing into my pillow while everyone else in the house is sleeping. I am left wondering if there a day that will come that will be marked in some way or other when I will be entirely useless. When the words won't come to take over my life every second, when I will be a child in a grown woman's body, an invalid dependant on other people, a caregiver's instinct? It's not the most natural feeling in the world to think about death all the time. Being morbid about it, imagining the funeral, what you will wear, what people will say in your absence, sing in the church, what colours the flowers will be that are placed on your grave?

Imagining your soul suddenly being displaced from your physical body, your heart, lungs, tissue, organs, all the biological elements, your spirit but sometimes it feels like the most natural vibration in the universe to me. Maybe because I'm a poet. I've got a lot of things on my mind. I've got a lot of things to say. I've got the time. I'm born to play with meaning, the English language, trivialise and over-emphasise the importance of this word or that and translate the light energies of a word into something much darker. Picture this. Visions shrouded in varying shades of black if you will. A blurry vision, totally out of focus, features not quite there as if someone forgot to take his or her finger off the lens and then slowly, slowly coming into view.

Today we're just being the Abbott's. My mother is drunk with spirit, talking in tongues under her breath, spitting the words out as if they were olive stones licked with salt. My father is pensive and looks as if he is about to cry. My brother is secretly laughing at all of us. My sister is working in a bank in another city, far away from the 'home fires' and 'stony pitfalls' that I have to keep putting out. I treasure these times. Life is good and I have never been better. (I'm a treacherous liar, a deceitful type of person, a 'fake', a poser, two personalities intertwined, battling it out. The 'extrovert' wearing the 'introverted me' out. Don't believe a word I say.) Today has been another great escape. The world rushes around me and whirls inside my head alongside with Woolf, Plath, Sexton and Winehouse. I'm inside my head again and perhaps the only dark times that I've ever experienced from my early twenties to my early thirties is the time I spent in hospital. It smells like rain. It's in the air. It has been all this afternoon.

Running on Lithium

Head made of stone sound the alarm for here hallucinations abound like driftwood, a gull sweeping through the sky overhead. In the photograph, her skin is as dark as dry blood as she stands in her white dress. She is the virgin bride on the surface. Is she happy standing next to her groom for her features communicate nothing to me? But her groom is smiling in the picture while the path to my heart lies in ruins. It's a path that reflects my standing in society. I am unmarried at thirty, having born no children from a womb that spirals in a rush of air, an echo of a flurry of blood for five days. When I speak now, it is in whispers in the company of other women who have crossed the boundary from youth into wifedom and motherhood effortlessly. I have been left behind and books, reading only gives up so much to the intellect of a woman (I have learned that this is not what other women covet).

It is a hollow and empty existence that I am engaged in, what am I living for then if not to spread myself across the flame of the dead, yielding myself to the flesh of their book histories. Once there were altered states of imagination and they now become mine to claim. To shut myself in when the world becomes cold, to commit myself to hide away, no matter how unbearable it becomes it still feels like home. It is a life to live even if it is always winter agents that come upon me. Ah, my comrades, they comfort me in my skin's glowering pose and that which is my sanctuary, where I lay my head to rest, to rejuvenate my senses that informs the psychology that I lead with. The canvas of the sun that breaks me like vultures and death.

The sun is silent over the sea mocking me while gliding across my shoulder blades like the falling water of a waterfall. Just as there is a miracle of life in seawater so there is in translation. She eats like a bird keeping all her secrets to herself like the surface of carrion passing triumphantly into blue oblivion where closure is self-imposed like the intimacy of letters in a novel language as thin as the width of a thread all thumbs. The weight of water has lightness in it. I've endured her harvest, my sister's time away from me, and the fact that summers have stolen her away from me. It has emptied my heart of wonder, of spells, locked me instead into building a wall around me, where I wait for her in silence. I wait for her to release me from the voice inside my head that has carried me from our childhood years, now to our passage as grown women. She has taught me to hold onto the familiar, the passing of the heavier moments slipping into time, pools, and curves of momentum and motion.

She is the land that time simply forgets to acknowledge. She seems to perfect everything. Her being is not as wooden as mine and her manners are not as stiff, her words are not strange and challenging. Words do not cure her as they do me instead my sister fills me up with meaning, with her marked pure rituals that came on the brink of her womanhood. Time has marked us as a minority, liberated us from a scheming mother, a quiet and gentle father. Now our parents have faded into the background like voids in the inner space of a lucid dream.

Flowers infect thoughts of death in the cemetery bittersweet like rage, a strange, demented vocabulary as if it were the memory of ill health. My emptiness dies with the dawn and finally calm I heal old wounds. I call this progress, obstacles and challenges have ceased to exist for me because all I see when I dig is the blade of the sun, and I have to endure for there is no other way out of the abyss except to jump over the black edge.

If I was writing an anthem for the youth where would I place meaning, how would utopia fit, the missing link, the most primal of screams, the poverty of the mind, that great divide between place and time. Where would a helpless poet transformed by ripples of a half-life of drowning in garlic, the familiar, the discovered plate find herself? Where would the poet frightened to death to be smitten, who instead embraces to be cured of it and having deciphered enough of it in lovely words threaded through her head realize that the world is not her home? It is only a meeting point where the courage for the broken is exposed and where it no longer mocks immortality, marriage or takes possession of physical space in an agonizing waiting game. Female poets see things in interiors, as instruments that can cut through the blue, the picture, and details of what a house means. For them, it's a song.

And when I fell in love the feeling was like the wind-song-wind-skin in birches, throughout the branches of the tree brushing strands of my hair into my face. Love felt like a great escape but when he left the hospital, he took the love with him and I became a stature of a woman, fearless, cold and heartless. I had notches on a belt. When I walked in the park it was not wilderness yet. It was only wilderness that I had to transcend in imagination. In a way it was love and in another way it was just a picture of love going up in flames, going up in smoke. I pocketed them all like silver keys calling them my dream keys for the future.

But doesn't everyone live in a dream world? They don't live like me with lithium. Catching tales of love with lithium. So, I stare at my reflection. The messy and dirty unkempt hair and tell myself, that smile suits you well. It's a ghost of the past sinking back into childhood where you made negotiations of the sea with your sunflower-yellow bucket and brick-red spade, your cone dripping on your sandy foot. And later the grammar and spells of gifted stars will rise above dunes like scrolling parachutes. But now it feels like winter. As if it has been winter all my life. Everything is dying around me. It feels as if I am dying to let go.

In my nightmares, there is the Mysterious Skin of a Haunted Street. All my old haunts figure. A school hallway, walking to school, in a classroom with a hated teacher, a friend's sweet face, the bully I feared the most on the playground. Going up then down is no fun. Really it was just a basket of hell as if I was sitting in the dark by myself watching bad television.

Every day at the hospital, I walk from room to room in the ward. It is a day in recovery. It can inspire. You're free to dream. No one can say anything if you do. The bright lights of the big city can hardly be seen from anywhere on the grounds. High walls and trees shield me. You can go from feeling like the most capable human in the world and then when that goes you feel extraordinarily incompetent, the introverted nature of being ill assumes fierce control and you are left retiring and docile, cooling your heels. My bright shouts draw a red line of emotional self-destructive behaviour through me. It doesn't take much to get me to a plane of being piloted by the life lessons depression leaves me with. There is something of a sweet dream about it. I've grown to love to fall into that sleep. It's a skill.

Sometimes you think the journey of the illness renders you invisible like air in your addiction for the tiny ball of golden light of health. So even if you're self-conscious of any small mistake you make, it makes you feel beautifully humanoid as if you weren't constructed by glorious organs, perfect tissue, cells, platelets, blood and bone and the image of genes in a jungle of veins. The doctors would like to think of change from being ill to an undeniable state of physical wellness was instant but I think that happened for the most part only in their dreams. Here, in this nameless, shapeless country, there were scenes of looking out into darkness' badly drawn addiction, and the act of alcoholism that had played a role in someone's life, a life of a family. Sufferers and victims and survivors bonded over a meal, gossip, the chit-chat of small talk. We were all joined together in the pursuit of becoming an outpatient. Of escaping what so easily we had come to think of as a route to follow to reality, normalcy.

I was a discoverer of the fractured known and the terrible force of the unknown. The flow I had to come to grips with clasped battle lines. For the most part, I felt lost like a pin in a pincushion, snow falling and given

20

room to grow to spread itself across the landscape. The jewel of mental health is to keep your spirit intact. You are at the mercy of the honesty of the illness. You're always curious to succeed even though you're at your most fragile. Humanity, normality still had the power to seduce. I had not completely abandoned that trail of thought. Hunger and hell became equals. The colour of the day was usually intensely blue (when I felt the depression articulate its nightmarish self), white (when I spent most of the day reading paperbacks, feeling acutely medicated and that it was the most unnatural feeling that I had ever felt) or red. That was when I couldn't put my rage and frustration and pack it into the life force of words. The only thing I could do was store it up in reserves. It gave me energy. But that energy was temporary like a fuse that blows or a spark.

When I left the hospital all I wanted to do was read books that doctors had written about depression, that pharmaceutical companies printed in their bright little pamphlets filled with colour and magazine models demonstrating 'sadness', 'family life affected by depression' and the symptoms. I could tick them all off one by one. In no uncertain terms, I was depressive. I read books on depression in which the detailed, uncompromising text left me reeling and scribbling away with a compelling and affecting urgency. I picked up memoirs or books on the lives of creative people who had suffered just like I had. I always found a vision, a better version of myself being reflected back at me.

The bottom of depression sinks further and further away into an abyss of nothingness. There is nothing I can do about it except stare into space until my eyes hurt and start to water or close them and wish the spell away. Once I was a city type of person rushing everywhere I needed to go but it soon paled. Poetry never did. And although poets were people whose lives were often not sanguine or bliss I believed in them, worshipped them. I discovered there were walls everywhere. To keep me in, protect me, to keep the death of me out.

21

I watch my weight constantly as if I'm under surveillance. I pick at my food. Nothing is good for me. I swear I eat in little bites as if it would help me in some way as if there is no dietician watching over my shoulder at the portion size. I don't keep it down for long. My throat burns as I run water in the bathroom. Nothing is nourishing or filling enough. To me, I never had a healthy relationship with food. I devoured the heaps of food on my plate with delight, savouring every crumb. All through high school, I was skinny. But the world when it turns on me soon everything begins to hurt like the plague.

Why couldn't all my eccentricities translate itself into something that was not touched by madness? But there is a powerful triumph in all of this – I can still write. It is my Source.

I wished I could shrug off blood, sweat and tears in high heels, with alluring self-confidence in an office space like my sister. But that is not me. It would not increase my knowledge of this planet; make me worthy of being in competition with my contemporaries.

It is disheartening feeling, thinking that you are never good enough. Never perfect. It came from the gilded cage of childhood and the reward of that had already shown up in my life. Already I had convinced myself I was less than zero, just a blurred negative. Imagine thinking so little of yourself that you thought being self-destructive was redemptive in some way.

When the world went black and the sky became hard, wrapped in stone, magic would course through me, my fingertips tingling, promising me a slight reprieve.

Into the Black

10

I am wearing ribbons in my hair. Today is my birthday and there are presents hidden with paper I can't wait to unwrap with trembling fingers. There are children running around and screaming, kicking the legs of their chairs underneath the dining room table that is covered with the birthday spread. Death by cakes that is the price. I can taste it in my mouth, review it in my head, and feel it all sinister suspiciously in my blood. It is all coming back to me now. My mother, is she sad or glowering at my father across the room? Is he sad or the picture of health? I have eyes that can see. Can't the eyes of a child see everything? The butterflies are so pretty. I can't bear to tear through the wrapping. It's a belt but I smile. It's a hard smile. I don't care what Anita says although Anita is my best friend. I have known Lynne longer because her parents are friends with mine. My parents have always taught me that it is the thought that counts. I stare at the flowers. I am sharing everything with Eve, my sister. Today is her birthday also. On my fifth birthday my aunt, my mother's sister played host while my mother was in labour at the Livingstone with Eve. Everything since childhood has been down the road or a few minutes' walk or an art not to fail or achieve, achieve, achieve, church, birth, high school, the park. There are other children here that I don't know. I don't speak to them. They are eating my cake. My mother is talking to them, asking about which school they go to, what grade they are in. She is wearing a pink dress with spaghetti-thin straps and sandals with heels. The dress has white polka dots on. She is much more animated with them than she is with me. She is smiling and laughing, asking them, these strangers in their party dresses who are parading across my mother's garden, oh-so-serious with their dark hair in long plaits if they are having a nice time, if they would like anything more to eat or to drink. If only she would pay attention to me. Everything about today is too bright, harsh, grating, working on my nerves. The sun, for instance, a girl's laughter (who is older than me), the energy from all the traffic in the house, the line for dessert. My mother has the brightness of two suns. Her hair flows around her face, her perfume in a cloud and as her foot hits the sandal it makes a squelching, sucking sound. I am free to do what I want. So, I choose to be alone. This is my day. Everyone else that I do not go to school with or play with in the afternoon are my mother's guests but all the girls seemed to have paired up with each other. They stand on the lawn looking bored, watching me the birthday girl and whispering secrets to each other. My sister, Eve, is still too small to play or to understand what the day really means. The boys are playing a rough and tumble game of hide-and-seek. Then it is time for the ice cream. The adults are going to play a video, something suitable for the younger generation, a cartoon. I can never remember what happens to my father when all this 'playing' is going on. There are never uncles on my birthday. My mother is not in the kitchen with aunts and older cousins arranging pies, finger food for a small army of neighborhood children or pouring wine in glasses for the adults mingling around the house. The uncles only come to drop their children off and then they are on their way again in their shiny cars pressing a creased note or a silver coin into my hand and kissing or rubbing the top of my head. I usually eat too much until my stomach hurts but there's the video. It is Looney Tunes, my favorite. I look around for my mother but she's not there. Eve is sitting too close to the television. I know that if I touch her, the golden child, she will yell and my mother would probably come running to see what is wrong and take me out in front of everyone. I feel lost and already I feel as if it is being stored up for a time when it will be of use, useful not to me but to other people.

15

Fifteen candles. There is nothing splendid about youth, growing older, feeling lost, unaccomplished and insecure. It just hurts, it hurts, it hurts. There is only the dreaming, the vision of escaping into marriage and having children that sticks. I am on that road of a poet who writes of madness and illness, the sweetness, the sweat of other people's lives. You wouldn't like me if you really knew me, knew who I was under lock and key, behind closed doors, poison flowing through my veins, pressure and stress touching the fragile core of me. The trophy doesn't feel, look real to me. But it is mine for a whole day and night before I have to return it. My name will be on it next year. For the first time in my life, I feel the pulse of those two words put together, creative writing. I am set on another course, meeting Fugard, reading English novelists in the library during a break in the school day, winning a role in the house play but in all that rush it is still quite never enough. I am programming Adam, my brother. He has to be prepared for war. We can hear them at night in their bedroom behind the closed door. Maybe we would have been better off pretending that they were moving furniture around at night instead of fighting, gloves off, anything goes, bitterness flying through the air followed by mock defeat, tantrum after tantrum, hysterics and the glowing seed of madness. I'm not going to cry. I'm not going to cry. I'm not going to cry. This is what I write about in an essay for school. I stay up the whole night into the early hours of the morning writing it because I have left it for the last minute. I write about the Holocaust. A young wife looking for her husband at a train station. It is different now from the beginning of the war when human beings were being transported like cattle, animals. These are survivors and she, the woman, the protagonist of my story, is looking for a family member or members. She imagines that her husband is still alive after Auschwitz and Bergen-Belsen. She is mad with grief. She is mad. But she believes because she has survived then so must he. I don't know how to end the story. In the end, I decide on ending it with a flashback to the house they first lived in when they were married and the roses she grew at the back of the house. Living through the internal, warped struggle of pain is easier to bear if you have read stories of pain and mental anguish in books or the newspaper or watched television. I didn't call it 'female suffering' then. I didn't know what to call it.

'It' was just surrounded overwhelmingly with disbelief and fog that for the most part was more than temporary and a saying that I chanted over and over again inside my head, giving it ample room to breathe, to exist. Nobody can hurt as much as I do. There are some parts of me that are broken. My heart, my family, my father and the pieces that are broken are lost forever. Worst of all, humans make a habit of forgetting the best parts. They are irretrievable and dark. But on the screen in front of me I can piece them back together again. They fit nicely. For a while they, although the words might seem odd, they stay put and then I say that will do. It gives me a kind of therapeutic pleasure. The opposite of truth is looking at the theory of it all blindly and looking at the theory of it all feels like running backwards. The theory of husbands and wives breaking up and then getting back together again, going over that is the easy part. They reach a milestone in their relationship, some sought of agreement or consensus and when finally, one reaches out to the other that spells the end, separation or divorce. But for the children instead of climbing hills merrily like other children their age, they will have to face mountains, climb the treacherous peak to get back to the start. They will also have to abandon the sides they choose but there was nobody to explain this to us, me, Eve and Adam when we were growing up. We didn't care. We made our own fun. We put on plays. We were each other's constant companions. We were happy. But the mechanism that kept our family together was going haywire. Our mother was a jumble of nerves. Our father, our hero and king was no longer the bright force in our lives that he once was. At night their bedroom door stayed shut and we couldn't even begin to imagine the personal torment and hell that he was going through.

17

The city reminds me of the sadness that I felt since I was a child. The Outsider, the loneliness, the ghost, the super rat catcher but that child is gone and in her place is a citizen of the world, a woman who needs to feel, to hear words of wisdom. A citizen who was taught that in everybody's life every moment of change is marked somewhat by pain, by a dream, by a faraway goal. The pages of my new journal are still fresh and new. I study them knowing that soon words will fill the pages, swim boldly, go where I have not gone before. Soon there will be words that will cauterise the page, leaving my head blank where it was once it was filled. There laid potential.

32

I have seen this in film, mental illness, the repercussions of hell, suffering and in the madness of men they are the creative thinkers, philosophers, called brilliant and genius, troubled in an unforgiving world. Those are the 'elite' names given to men. Did I need more explanation than that for the chronic mess I usually found myself in? But I never knew the precise moment when I felt different or moved differently or articulated something with more bravado than I knew I had. But people that I knew and sometimes that I was close to knew that I was different and wasn't afraid to tell me so. Most times they made a joke of it. I am sure perhaps they did not mean to sound cruel, unkind or like a bully on a school playground but that is how I interpreted it. It still makes me nervous when I meet new people. When I have to make conversation, I always want someone to save me from myself. Do I howl when I laugh or snort with derision? Everything feels like the opposite of sublime as if ants have got into the sandwiches in the picnic basket, as if I am covered in blood and people are staring. Female suffering is different from a man's rage and depression. They want to give their children what they did not have. They want to give their children what they longed for and wished for, what they desired as children and young girls before they became women and a picture, sometimes a mirror image of their own mothers. If a man is violent, a woman is emotional and sensitive. She has her own needs. For me to write was enough and for my mother it seemed that children and a large, spacious house to raise a family in was enough. But my father was not a violent man, a heavy drinker, a smoker, brutal towards my mother and I and my two siblings. He was warm and soft and a cuddly teddy bear. He had brown eyes and made us all feel safe when we were growing up. He rested a lot. When he came home from school (he was a principal at a high school), I would watch him sleep from the doorway always waiting for him to wake up and catch sight of me. And I would wait for him to embrace me. I would never catch him embracing my mother because she hated public displays of affection. Not in front of the children, I could imagine she probably hissed under her breath so many times, too many for my father to count until he stopped doing it. At night my father would work on his doctoral thesis in his study. We were not to play near the closed door or disturb him. You can't imagine all the difficulties I have had to go through, the ghosts I have to put up with and the order and normalcy and simplicity I crave. What does snow feel, taste like? Like any wet, cold thing, like rain? The dogs are barking. They are going mad in the distance. There is something in his voice that annoys me, irritates me so I turn the television off. It must stay off. I am restless so I do what I know so well. I read. How far is it to the next hour? Why the overexposed, the challenges, mercies, points of departure, the roast chicken, vegetable soup welcoming me home? It is the dead of winter that I want; that I left behind in Johannesburg. It was the winter that toughened me up. Cold turning in the air, holding still in the middle of traffic facing off for their line of attack of the destitute huddled over fires under the highways and bridges and squatter camps where there are no wet leaves and butterflies.

My sister seemed so cold and indifferent, aloof; she seemed to want to distance herself from us, the rest of the family as if she was made of brighter, harder, weightier stuff than the rest of us, as if it wasn't in her bloodline and the ladder of her genes to fail. We were weak, she was a saint. My reality for the better part of the day and sometimes the night was borderline as if I were part of a tribe of people that time forgot in blue interiors. Swimming in a pool of blue; as if the blue had the same consistency as ink in my eyes, the blue skin of the swimming pool against my skin and of course, the pale blue school floating overhead like a ghost in a machine. Only here I felt safe amongst other schoolchildren and mothers, swimming instructors, lifesavers and fathers. Nobody could tell I was different. I was a nameless citizen. My limbs sank into the cool water as if I was sinking into hollows of warm sand. Home was a hot mess. Only in water could I escape from that fuss. Forget my brother was locked in rehab, forget my sister never phoned to speak to me, forget that nobody ever phoned. That is what the writer works with – interiors, the dark and the lightest parts of it, the architecture of the formative years, objects around the writer's working manners.

What was left at the end or the beginning of the day was represented to me as light in a life force, a space to start from and a transition from a dream zone to a life lived in relative comfort. Away from the stresses of and from the different paths and roads I have taken, only I had access to the museum I had built up of all the negativity I had connected with and collected over my life experience. I wish it would be easier to explain things sometimes. This is what my mother does when she picks up a brush. A hairbrush, a toothbrush to put her 'other-face' on when she's off to church, a workshop at her church, to do service at the hospital, when she pushes off to a church meeting and then suddenly the love of God rises up in her when she dims her sweet pride, the rising panic and anxiety in the emotional screech of her hysterics as she makes waves all around us. She walks out with her heels clicking, glamorous and shiny, a smartly dressed Christian woman, her hair falling in dark brown curls around her face.

Everything about her is soft, her clothes sticking to her figure, the flame of red on her cheeks, smelling like powder and scent, freshly washed blow-dried hair. Everything about me is hard, hardened by spent energy, by wasted time, by doing nothing, by sleep, by engaging my intellect and by asking myself, 'If my mother really loved me, why would she say those things? Does she hate daddy? Is God punishing me, us, the family and why?' This is memory and bitterness at work in the walking wounded.

A Few Good Citizens

*Y*outh. Nothing about youth diminishes, about dying and culture. It is still a shock to the system when it arrives on the scenario, the scene of the volume of sky and a child caught in the drift of time, a storm is raging inside my head, deep inside me I am a still life, a figure whose reflection glitters. The dead do not speak of trivia. They no longer can bask in the orange disc of the sun with their infirmities and stiff upper lips, shielding their malnourished children who suck their gums in hunger, in thirst, waiting in a line that does not move, they wrap their arms around their mother's graceful neck, as graceful as a swan's. What does a poet see in this, what is revealed in this time and place, psychology and consciousness, how do certain words, the poet's imagination perform? There is still hope for this ravaged continent that is hurting so, it hurts to breathe, to think, to stare at this poverty, this nation in the face, are they too hungry to even think of revolution, their eyes can melt the hearts of stone in any scenery and anything that flows into and around their world, through their mouths, into their bodies is an elixir, even the spacious expanse of the sky above their heads. As they sit day in, day out they wait to live through their fate; do they feel hatred towards the God of this society?

Poverty. What warms their hearts, the impoverished, is it only the ancient traits of teachers and guides, things they know or poverty, that imperfect feeling of something missing that has molded them into the earthy creatures they are today, the drumming noises of the planes in flight, how close they have come to dying instead of being. What are they most grateful for? They will never know of the wings of a poet writing about prayer for hope for the continent of Africa, of my obsession of them, of the foreigners who descend like wolves, people trapped in a terminal, of my roots to the universe. The sun is silent over the sea, mocking me while gliding across my shoulder blades like falling water. Just as there is a miracle of life in seawater so there is in translation. Magic mother eats like a bird keeping all her secrets to herself like the surface of carrion passing triumphantly into blue oblivion where closure is self-imposed, as the intimacy of letters in a novel language as thin as the width of a thread, all thumbs. The weight of water has lightness in it. I wished for someone to end my sentences. Could we stop the sounds of falling rain if we weren't exposed to the song in it if we paid more attention to it like a dream? As hard as air, poised yet fragile, you, father, are mapped with fragile lines.

Adele. I've endured Adele's harvest, her fairytale feeling, her time away from me, the fact that summers have stolen her away from me, emptied my heart of wonder, of spells, locked me instead into building a wall around me, where I wait for her in silence to release me from the voice inside my head that has carried me from our childhood years, now to our passage as grown women. She has taught me to hold onto the familiar, the passing of the heavier moments slipping into time, pools and curves of momentum and motion of the land that time simply forgets to acknowledge. She seems to perfect everything. Her being is not as wooden as mine, her manners as stiff; her words are not strange and challenging. Words do not cure her as they do me instead, she fills me up with meaning, with her pure rituals that came on the brink of her womanhood. Time has marked us as a minority, liberated us from a scheming mother, a quiet and gentle father; they have faded into the background like voids in the inner space of a lucid dream.

Rivals. After Adele, I have realized that there is nothing ordinary about this land of rural countryside, the wild, the wilderness, commodity, routes of heat and dust high in the blue of the sky and the slow caress of the sweep of larva, the inhabitants' eyes like the dark. It's a land of calculated bullets, sensual young women, fierce youth, stifled judges and the white fingers of galloping mist. And for those that are city-born, educated, amongst the privileged few, the only information that they have about this land is what they read about in books. What they are pulled towards and pushed against in the plane of their consciousness. In other words, the lies they were told as children. We are made in our personal capacity to hope and there will always be a haunting beauty in that like stone and iron in earth, just like the stone, iron, fire in our blood, denizens of Africa in the copious movement of struggle against colonialism, against backlash, poverty, wealth, that great divide where boundaries lay unquestioned, tolerated at best. 'Smile,' you, magic mother, dew blinking in your eyes, in your black stockings, your tender physical body so different from mine, slender, health rushing through you pure and earnest said, but it hurt to smile.

Culture. The Port Elizabeth and Johannesburg of my childhood were far away from this. The cities I experienced as an adult were meaty and ghoulish that smelled like a vagrant imposing his presence, the smell of sour mildew, the residue of stains and the air of loneliness, homelessness, tragic circumstance and of being mocked, chastised on his person. A sourness on his breath of wine or something stronger like spirits that warmed the death of frozen him up on wintry nights, when it rained, the vagrant, a bone man with a lack of education and a bleak future teetering on the brink. Port Elizabeth, more town than city, more smear of a mouse than a wild, hirsute, obscene giant in its outlook than that great bustling beehive of a hub of a city, Johannesburg. Its people with their slogans tattooed on their chest working hard to pay their bills, to escape from their failures and triumphs being eyed in the workplace. The landscape of Port Elizabeth has an orange afterglow in the late afternoon – pollution from the factories on the industrial side of town. The people glow too but it is more internal. It is as if they are lit up from the inside by a flame. They're people who burn like a volcano, that fades into the night, marching onward, focused on their destination, complete, sated.

Time. The pear juice dribbling down my chin tastes sweet. I can imagine the look of love drifting into view for some of them, family, children and lovers, expectation meeting the rise of anticipation. It's nice out. Muse has a new name – children playing out on sunny roads. On waking there is the thought of the onset of age, of peeling back the layers of being, of nothing from the present to the scenic. Mostly for now I sit and write about my mother and father and the tears that came and went like ice in a waterfall staring right through me as it floods my mind's eye. There is something heroic about the day. About the people with their being and nerve fused to their vision of the day. If I were like them, I would turn into a green-eyed monster, Bluebeard. Even the flawed, the tarnished, the idiot, people who time forgot are loved. There's a period of growth even in silence, a pause between acts, stillness when you gather your thoughts in inner space. Code starts with me first, as soon as the destination becomes important so does the secret language of women, men, children, their angel tongue comes with this volcano rushing through my head, shadows drowning out the switches from the philosophy of a child to woman.

Pearls. There is a new and almost poetic intensity to my dreams now, where water holds me and currents flow through me with bright new energy, vibration and force. I am not the bride, the new wife. Instead, I am transfixed by the enigma of the generous, unbearable lightness and the darker strokes and dimensions of the profound world of words, glowing chronic illness. My father is not in perfect health, he is frail, and prayers have carried him through and he thinks he has to live through his pain, that he hasn't reached kismet. He has told us how he would like to go, he shared this with us, his children in a cemetery while placing half dead flowers on our grandparents grave, and perhaps the message had come from God and as we sat in the cold all I could see were trees stitched to the ground, lifted up, head high in the most deserted of all resting places, the green of the leaves fading away into the afternoon light with the change of the seasons. As I took my father's arm, I could feel the warmth of his blood under his jacket. The only thing that mattered at that moment was the three of us communing with the elements, clouds gathering overhead, other families paying their respects to relatives that had passed on. If people lived on the moon how they would ever begin to fathom justice for their loved ones if the universe's tides didn't turn.

Cut. The flowers infect thoughts of death in the cemetery bittersweet like rage, a strange, demented vocabulary as if it were the memory of ill health. My emptiness dies with the dawn and finally calm I heal old wounds. I call this progress, obstacles and challenges have ceased to exist for me because all I see when I dig is the blade of the sun, I have to endure for there is no other way out of the abyss except to jump over the black edge. Writing an anthem for the youth where would I place meaning, how would utopia fit, the missing link, the most primal of screams, the poverty of the mind, that great divide between place and time, a helpless poet transformed by ripples of a half-life of drowning in garlic, the familiar, the discovered plate, the poet frightened to death to be smitten, who instead embraces to be cured of it and having deciphered enough of it in lovely words threaded through her head realizes that the world is not her home, it is only a meeting point where the courage for the broken is exposed and where it no longer mocks immortality, marriage or takes possession of physical space in an agonizing waiting game. (Poets) female poets see things in interiors, as instruments

35

that can cut through the blue, the picture, details of what a house means, for them it's a song.

Art. If the sun didn't burn so bright in my eyes would I see angels falling from the sky wearing white robes? Head made of stone–sound the alarm for here hallucinations abound like driftwood, a gull sweeping through the sky overhead. Her skin is as dark as dry blood as she stands in her white dress, the virgin bride on the surface, is she happy standing next to her groom, her features communicate nothing to me but her groom is smiling in the picture, while the path to my heart lies in ruins, reflects my standing in society – unmarried at thirty, having born no children from a womb that spirals and whirls in a rush of air, an echo of a flurry of blood for seven days. When I speak now, it is in whispers in the company of other women who have crossed the boundary from youth into wifedom and motherhood effortlessly, and I have been left behind and books, reading only gives up so much to the intellect of a woman (I have learned that this is not what other women covet). It is a hollow and empty existence that I am engaged in, what am I living for then if not to spread myself across the flame of the dead, yielding myself to the flesh of their book histories, once their altered states of imagination now becomes mine to claim, to shut myself in when the world becomes cold.

Hands. To commit myself to hide away, (no matter how unbearable it becomes it still feels like home, a life to live even if it is always winter agents that come upon me. They are my comrades. They comfort me in my skin's glowering pose, that, that is my sanctuary, where I lay my head to rest, to rejuvenate my senses that informs the psychology that I lead with, the canvas of the sun that breaks me like vultures and death. In the middle of the night I fly away in my dreams and one night all I could see were black dogs, as black as a river barking madly. They were swathed in night air but before they descended upon me, I woke up. In another dream, I was praying for the madness in my world to end, (I could sense if I peeled the psychic skin back, there was a lesson of biblical proportions there). Wasteland, fog or clear skies my dreams smell like perfumed incense, feels like a feather in the palm of my hand, angelic choirs singing, open country, the playing fields of children; dreaming often feels surreal to me, is it a part of my real life or am I hallucinating or a woman in motion with pain written everywhere on my body in invisible ink, lonely is the heart of the poet, just another vision of winter, always searching for the truth inside of myself, inside my soul.

Family. What I remember about childhood is a child's fists painted with mud pies, adults with their bleak smiles swimming out of reach. Moon people do not have to speak of the volume of their loneliness in a human traffic wonderland. This is a story about that childhood. Parts are funny, there are some grim portraits, (about the grown-ups); most of all there is something pure about the life experience, the gems, the hopes, the dreams and the goals that inhabit the world of a child. With its walls made of infinite space I watched myself become more detached as I grew older, surer of myself. This is also a story about the other me, 'her'. How she left me wrung-out, a washed out pale like mysticism's shroud. From that thing, that skin of a telescope, books were my eyes and ears to the world, the adult world, and its core's pulse. And I learned I had to keep words like, 'Why are you sullen, something difficult?' to myself with resignation. 'Why do you burn like larva?'

Poets. Blistering, spirited sun dancing on the ground, how on earth did you get here? Why do you have that effect like some poet whose text is like a boomerang or pillars? It's as if you possess magical thinking with the planets, the moon in union around you. Who or what awakened you, brought you to an altered human consciousness? When children laugh, do angels above in heaven sing like the poet sings when he has seen signs of his wisdom in what he has written; through God's flute come prayers that we, humanity must take cognizance of. Just like there are kingdoms in manuscripts, so there are in the seasons, in the plant and animal world, the ocean-sea, so death finally begins in the poet's life itself as his vanishing slowly begins to form and take shape, as he grows older and his body begins to grow soft, infirm, perhaps his hands are crippled with arthritis, lonely he spends his days in meditation, introspection, reading, wishing he could turn back the clock. It is the sun that reminds him of what he was like as a child, as a boy he was a scavenger, a warrior, playing at war with his boyhood friends, he is still oblivious to youth and culture shock, to the highs and lows of mania, meeting the beautiful woman who is going to be his not so perfect wife with her own depression belly up; they both had things to learn from each other, hostility, silent treatment, with only small children to set their souls at peace. What if the sun was the center of the universe, what if my father asked himself at some point if he had made her the sun in his?

Milestones. As the sun sets, I am caught wishing I was a child again with that festive, birthday air around her, that time has not taken its toll on me, middle age was not rolling in, that language was still a strange tongue for me and that I still painted fish in Sunday school. But tonight, instead I will meditate, connect to the earth and forget about the small kittens we found a year ago, striped bundles of warmth falling into the air to be caught in my hands under fluorescent lighting in the garage, forget what any rogue or solitary wined man would mean by a stare. Tonight, I will push past the roughness of the galaxy. Fast forward my response to all my hurt and regret that could fill the oceans of the overworked sea. This is when my thoughts turn and I remember Adele floating on air, so beautiful and elegant. Skin pale with no lines showing through yet. No cracks, not ancient, with invincible youth on her side. A rose in each cheek, scent in her rinsed hair, a winter guest in a world, a universe, on a planet in a Johannesburg all snowy almost overnight.

Imagination. When you left this world turned on me, crippled me and left my heart in a frail knot, tangled in the mirth of obsession towards possession, form, force, a waking flame and the arrows of a being of light. They were contagious as a rolling shift in tides, as I progressed towards you lost in the land, shades and country of Jane Austen. I basked in the glory of her elements, sampled incandescence and fragile quiet. If fish could only live on air as I do. Instead, they breathe the juice, the veil of fire on an expedition from sea to land before they're completely erased from sight like you have been, leaving me quite ill, inconsolable against the invincible cosmos I searched this house, turned it upside down until all my thoughts were black and impoverished. How can I banish the song in my clothed hunger, my still, patched, dark thirst? The climb has been a cold one to bear. Night has ravaged me senseless so that I've taken to medicine which has transitioned me from ancient death to the tree of life, made me march to the sound of cars and dogs barking in bursts, the background of the vein of rain, the symmetry of stars and the silence of a planet when the night falls. If only you were here within reach, smelling of roses, the bite of my prize poem, kind, alive, not in flight.

Halfway. Meeting in the middle is a force to be reckoned with. Where do Adele, Godwin and Isobel meet if not meant to in the aftertime of city-people? There is something heroic about the day, any day because aren't battles fought continually, yet people emerge (there is evidence of this) more or less resilient, flexible, sometimes harder to crack or hurt. There are those whose interior is impenetrable. There is something to be said about the people with their being and nerve fused to their vision of the day.

Godwin. Blue reminds me of the ocean, a female on a suicide mission, the end and the edges of the sky, warmth sucked inside of me. I was that girl with the fake bonhomie in blue jeans and blue buttoned-down shirt, melting in the heat and dust because of my long sleeves. You rode up to the hill with me in your car with a tape playing in your stereo. I came to your house. I sat on your bed. I watched you carefully, watched you flow into and around your objects, your books, your pictures, your art, your shoes, all your electronic technical stuff and your 'things', especially when you came into contact with your mother. I didn't want to be in your way but I was. And the rush of what I felt was invincible. Already I didn't fit (I was a square peg in a round hole) and didn't have a clue how to fit or how to behave amongst culture shock and a significant rival. Then you decided the manner to unravel another country.

Emptiness. There I sat a little Buddha resting, little Buddha made of stone or one of Helen Martin's menageries; me keeping you company and what its flesh implied to me was frightening, authentic in its own way but frightening in comparison to the clouds scissoring through the drift of summertime air. I paled while you were flexing, impressing upon me the onslaught of the daily grind of challenges you faced. And for that afternoon 'in the other room', I was in your cave where only the invited guest ever set foot by your order and command. You thought I could help in some way, mentor you in some capacity. But kismet was sealed and I was trapped with your name already a pearl on my lips. In retrospect, it was tragic the way I suited up for my list of companions, the strategic cycle of them that I planned with logic precision but more or less it didn't come down to the fire or how the flame burned. It came acutely with half-dreaming loosed on me.

Creation. I could imagine you walking around in your white socks, shuffling in that big house eating, talking, laughing, singing or drinking wine with your family in the evenings with a light meal. It was already crowded. It was plain to see there was no room for me. But you are gone like the English teacher who really was English, imported from the great, wet and cold Britain, like the one who got away with his wife carrying a child in her belly, the one who worked for the BBC, the producer, the writer, the poet, the 'spy' who sold vitamins. All left me tangled in mist and vague observation, mental anguish and ill health. Unfortunately, love never leaves you or what your senses, what you experienced in life during that time completely. It serves as a healthy lesson to reinforce something, a fact of life that you will never forget that came to you as a blessing in disguise.

Drama. But for the craft of creation, 'it' to be a blessing you must have been interrupted post-crisis by a spiritual plane. If I think of those 'teachers' who have guided me temporarily it is to distraction, a race against time and I am in that room again, the world in my eyes gone, launched in orbit in an outer space, a divine realm navigated by loss, always loss that feels like being caught in snow. For D. H. Lawrence love is good enough 'so long as it didn't fizzle out in talk'. The trouble with men is that they don't remember. They're not built that way. They're made of portions meant to be reading the signs, gathering them up of what will follow after the situation or conflict with the female or females in their male-dominated arena. Men are spoilt by the choice they have in women who will love

41

them. It is the woman who will fall for the dreams in that man and the goals he has set aside for himself. It is a fable as ancient as the parables. These demigods have taught me that to eat is to live. It has taken me some time to retaliate, to feed on and off secret comfort, cast the sun out, me the brief discoverer that my ignorance was no longer bliss and that enlightenment triumphantly entitled me to regard men as the enemy. I discovered this thought in all of them. Before I could move, they wanted to know what was the effort for, why that variation in my tone, why I did not speak. I was so good at the latter that it became my truth. I could wing it and fly. I had no need for speech or drama.

Self-worth. Peace is a country, an apt pupil in rain or a cement garden. It tastes like warm plums. You taught me that all life is temporary, it's a moment of being and the road's ever-present and thickening blackness coming out to meet blind me only served as company, which I would be bound to for eternity, although it would require some delicate adjustment. The cutout act of that would fit me like a second skin. I was made to understand children even if they were not my own. This muse set in stone. A poetess conceived like a Greek goddess, more imaginary than real, head inspired by the committee of nightmares, insomnia, cigarettes, the motion sickness of the scar of loneliness, the manic energy of staying up all day, all night. Being put into action until what was left of them was just the vision bleeding into the landscape of evening's shades, the vision of units of memory rolling like a wave until it made a statement. I have always been able to see you like I have seen the alphabet, help in therapy. I have made it my cause and platform to write out of defiance, more importantly, because it makes you go underground until you love yourself.

Isobel. Isobel was an exceptional learner in the shop. She had been promoted to assistant manager. Isobel's, her outer 'skin', (a play at subterfuge), her clothes were an expression of her anonymity (in that crowd so she wouldn't feel alien). Johannesburg set in modern times is now a place where being human is an experiment carried out in the ongoing black depths of the night air in the city. The man in this picture is watching the woman in the same picture as he tells her something to impress upon her his genius in the world. The curl of her lip on the rim of the glass, the way she tidies and fusses with her hair, tucking it away behind her ear is encouraging his bravado and play. The way she does it is sensual. His lips are wet and as the evening progresses, he becomes braver. She leans into him because the music is too loud, the conversations from the tables around them and then he begins to stroke her arm with his index finger. She sighs. 'I'm so tired. We were so busy today.' Is he listening to her, she wonders? Is he focused on the final outcome of the evening? She shivers and turns her head away. 'Where do you work? Is it far from here? What time do you knock off? Maybe we can meet up halfway somewhere. I usually like to come here in the evenings.'

Melting. The drink is beginning to take effect on her. Does it show, she wonders and this guy is starting to play, asking her questions, personal questions and begins to sound more and more like trouble to her? She begins to think that this was a bad idea, a very bad idea but he had genuinely seemed nice but why all these questions. She doesn't want to go to a hotel or his house. What she wants is to get out of this, this mess. He wants her to think that he doesn't think the same as other men do. He respects her and somehow, he must get that across in his tone of voice in his conversation with her. That must count for something in this mating game but before she is caught in his snare, she glares at him (she knows what he wants and hates this 'lie' but it is not that late, the brightness of the

43

day has faded (like her resolve is fading fast before this hunter)) and before he buys her another drink she excuses herself to go fix her hair and makeup. She does not like to drink but men look at her differently when she does. They notice her. The same man is waiting for her response to him. Men hungry for women frequent these bars and upmarket restaurants. Their need for the attention and admiration of the woman is never satiated. But first, he has to talk and listen, play this little game that he doesn't sometimes have the energy for.

Volcano. There's nothing cute about it. Men, don't they get easily bored, enraged even when their feelings are not reciprocated? Their line is, 'I have spent money on you. You owe me something.' Their eyes seem to say, glowing with their pent-up exertions of the evening. The woman, hurt, holds onto the disaster, flirts with it, (it is too late for her to make up some excuse to leave), nursing a comeback with the alcohol generating warmth. And when it comes it is usually these words with a luminous effect. 'You don't own me. Leave me alone.' An ugliness or near-hysteria coded in her voice.

Lament. I have met all the Isobels and Adeles and Godwins of the world that I want to meet in my lifetime. I have had to fathom them all out like the dark, their soul-pieces and say, leave me to it.

Kenneth's Feats of Pretty Things

To keep my mind away from you, teacher, to stop it from enthralling me, to keep the knowledge of you clean, as pure as the collection of lost and found, an uneducated volcano, impatient smoke and the voice of denial. I have become a series of pounding satellites in orbit, the reminder of skinned knees from meeting the pavement, scary broadcasts on the evening news with the words coming out effortlessly from research. That is where I'm coming from, an illuminist. Fear from childhood gone. Fear from a hobo's eye. Troops in hardship just an imprint burned on my brain. My bedroom has become my throne room. Here I have turned hours into a spotlight on loves, death, eternity, daughters and mothers. Alluring lands of magic and wonder, the enduring secrets of my heart have become my playmates. When I was a child with growing pains in my mother's house, enchantment was internal in dreams and journeys like water in wild places but after that season passed, that phase of my life, with the elegant curve of the winter sun in the sky, water became more fluid in streams and rivers and for the passage of time that I have known you, I know that there will come a day, a time of night when it will stop flowing from memory. Gravity was the only thing holding you and when the world was a white blanket of snowy mist you kept me company on those walks to and from school even though you did not walk beside me.

When my comprehension of you standing in front of the class, in your thin, pale shirt, darkly serious, when you were an empire on your own, I blinked and in a volunteered instant you were gone from my domain. Your voice was like a rite to me. Awareness of that voice brought me to your location, grilled me. It made me feel as if I had taken a bullet. I had a body double stuck in the perfect time machine. It gave me a warm feeling (the same feeling I got when I heard thunder peeling through the dark, the night air's skies), a feeling not for the fainthearted. You taught me about humanity from contextual reasoning, the black alphabet that is written on my ego, the ego of all poets and the female wanderlust.

I find in that still life the quiet the writer's soul longs for, the silence that is like a terrible scar before it marks itself as refuge, it manages itself as an intense feeling of joy, a hunting ritual, a spiritual rite, an extraordinary state of calm in that identity of all identities that is created without borders, joints where there is always a motivating space for beautiful learning. I often wonder at the family, the background, the self-assessment of writers and think to myself that voices male and female will fuse eventually in a sacred contract and the storytelling that will emerge, will emerge (with a universe that has become second-nature to me) as a collective, as a community, as a commodity, writers writing, eliminating the most unnatural. We will prosper, cross that universal threshold together, changing, seizing the spinning web of history, becoming penning confessors of the intimate, we will commune with the virgin birth of interpretation with the anonymous, the creative myth, gift and the creative impulse falling into whole infinity. Should we be calling ourselves plain and simply just 'writers'? Which is the most authentic way of describing ourselves? Why should we label ourselves? A home of writers is a profound community like mind will often meet like mind. These were ideas I was battling with even then as a learner. A community of writers is a home wherever you find yourself in the world and because of Mr English, the master of English, my teacher I have become more truthful, a reader, a writer, a faithful poet. 'You' seem to fade away to noun and pronoun. What becomes of his, he, him, he's? I am left to fill the blank spaces, all the details. I stare at him from my desk. He wears thin shirts. He's unmarried. He's published a book for schoolchildren. All of these notes of information I store them up as I come to learn of them through rumours and hearsay as I do my secret love for my English-English teacher. He takes the bus and every day he can be found in a thin stream of schoolchildren walking from school to the centre of town, construction all around a parking lot. His fingers are the fingers on a guitar. So, his words become my words. Everything about him is electric. Remembering how futile everything seemed to be in the beginning when I had first found myself in this country. How miserable and homesick I had been it had all been worth it. He held words like a pearl or a shiny bead on his tongue and after he launched them into the air, he would swallow them whole. In my mind's eye, in the time he takes with the short story he reads aloud with expression and the questions he poses to different students, while he walks around the class, I devour the characters and the lines of poetry he recites is like a flame. He constructs fire, cats, young love, symmetry, sleet beautifully. It is almost as if I can feel the young heroine's passion. I am that young heroine cast aside in youth, that most high feeling not reciprocated, not given a chance to develop, transition into maturity. Secret love crushed, just a seductive experiment, a material concept for my wish-fulfilment ideals. There are molecules in everything. Even in Kenneth Smith's feats of pretty things he left behind. Skirts hiked up high, brushing against thigh, knees quite bare and long-sleeved white blouse, dark heads bowed over their readers, textbooks and binders. There was no warning that he would leave to teach at another school. So, it was something that took me by surprise when the new English teacher introduced himself. And now I was alone again without my 'ally' and it scared me because without him I no longer felt quite so invincible but more vulnerable. With the newfound loss came a change of season and I was flung into the winter light, into the hush of the soft, secret places of mothers and daughters.

Stars far off were whirling away at a swift glance with a pure, pale rush on this sleeping planet. Loss I learned bound you, the beautiful, the fragile and the rare and in the swan-like wonderland of this ancient countryside I remembered playing with dolls, the wounds children would leave behind that mushroomed, exploded like torture and that was slow to vanish. I melt into the river of darkness all around me in my dreams in this foreign country. (Swaziland is a swimming goddess on the end of my tongue), darkness like a decorative shroud covers me up from view until it seems I can hardly breathe but it is for my own good. It is to protect me from witches, vampires and werewolves. No more Mr Smith to protect me.

The other learners are more unforgivable yet less conniving and wild than other girls and boys I've come across. At first, they're like iced places of cold comfort rush or where you'll still be able to find a winter chill or breeze in spring air collecting dust. There was part of me that was scared of growing, celebrating another birthday, going through with the ceremony of all of that, scared that others would see me, sense that I was crippled in some way like a Down syndrome babe with a pale face like a moon gutted out that hinted at gods, that would leave a mark on me in society, that others would make fun. So, this is where my conversations with Buddha and God come in. I found in silence a song of love and the older I seemed to get the more that song seemed to give way to a theory of flight and I simply came alive to see what escape there was in it. Like shooting stars falling from the night air's skies orbit to the earth, they do not journey gently in dreams. Mr English, Kenneth Smith is still three suns exploding in my face and in his leave of absence I found that there could be a continual sense of healing found. Healing multiplied in name, identity, space and peace of mind. When he was no longer there, I would pretend I was writing to him in class, that he would get my letter, and that I could touch the fine-fine threads of his silver hair, trembling, that I could run my hands through it, pinch a tuft through my fingers. I would write to him in equations, promising solutions, graphs, essays, and assignments. I knew I was only clutching at straws and that nothing would ever come of it.

I was still a relatively young girl on that stretch of open road reaching emotional maturity, a spiritual existence, a sense of my physical being and the sense of the more experienced, less giving world around her and that I was as present as present was present in the abstractedness of a painting. I did not yet know that I was capable and that as a woman I was capable of many things. The female wisdom that I collected in youth would only be put to use later on in life. At this stage it is in the beginning levels of a more striking multi-faceted approach, it is infinitely far-reaching and more powerful than a male's. It was a world that I didn't quite feel up to the challenge of taking head-on, made up of chiefs and tribes of men that I didn't feel I completely belonged to naturally.

I still wished for him but not in seeing things in diamonds and kisses, rubbing it clean away with the back of my hand. I wished to be united against this world with someone who could speak for me, protect me against the harsher, darker elements, harmful dimensions. Already I found an eternally formidable promise, a gap in falling into a tangled web of darkness visible – depression, only it wasn't called depression. Then I called it 'being quiet, being slow, soaking up the sun, sucking hollows into warm chocolate Easter eggs melting in my hands, dreaming of the syllables unfolding in my imagination of haiku, everyone knows that I am different and in learning to be different it took the shape of the Hudson. And when I began to write for English class Kenneth Smith was always in the frame of my mind. I pictured him making his way through the papers, marking them in red pen and finally until he came across my paper in the bunch, there is where he would finally align his vision with mine. At first glance perceptions are normality not borderline or bipolar; they're usually just realities of light and energy. I felt an undeniable (yet also unattainable sense) of magic drawing in his dance of movement and on the contemporary as he made his way between the desks in the classroom.

Memory, memory, memory could hurt the eyes, could pierce the heart away in tune to their own Hiroshima, could half-drown you in a bucket.

There between my pages he would find a poetic ministry, meaning, shielding me (and my secret forever) and standing solid at the same time behind my descriptive words. He made everything sound pretty and as fragile as glass in class, where he stood magnificent and cold up-front reciting poetry out loud, completely detached from the reaction that was being raised in the crush of my schoolgirl's heart. It had brought me much-undisclosed joy to watch this adult male in my hemisphere. We would have 'conversations'. We would talk about books. My first choice had to be William Styron's *Sophie's Choice*. I could imagine reading some of his own work, praising him or telling him what to rework, blushing that I could be that brave. Back home before I had left when I had been a townie with the infinite sea in my backyard, before I discovered 'the' Sylvia Plath, her husband Ted Hughes and their baby daughter Frieda in a poem in a time and place unlike any other I had ever experienced, in a country that time had for the most part seemed to have forgotten. I stood on the beach, the wailing wind in my hair feeling as if the earth had been chilled by the inclement weather. Smooth, clean, washed stones, gulls softened feathers find its place channelled. They scrape against sand. On the beach, my mother blazed a path past me, her mouth set in a grim, determined line. History only keeps repeating itself if you give it permission. Those are my words, nothing borrowed or blue about it.

For it, histories, to permanently dissolve you have to have reason. A woman, a girl rather waiting to fall in love, waiting for a suitor, a suitable companion is like an accident waiting to happen, a steak and kidney pie falling out of the sky into the lap of a devout drinking-tea-strictly-tea-with-crumpets Englishman. If I didn't love him then, what seems a lifetime ago, I wouldn't be listening to music that makes me dance now, be the circumspect keeper of children's dreams; believe that not having any of my own at this stage of my life tastes like chicken, that it is neither here nor there but it makes me feel a little better if 'it' comes with potatoes. I am a better poetess, better at being present to have known him in the jungles of the cities I have lived in so far.

Diary of an insomniac

I want you to feel the cold like I do, weep as I do, make sense of the senseless world around you like I do. I want you to imagine the unbearable lightness, futility, looseness of things past holding you back, courage for the broken with the frame of mind of coming out of the dark. Imagine the ghosts that congregate around you in interiors, the print of wet leaves spilling over, the goddess-mother. Imagine the anonymous millions eking out a living, living on borrowed time, borrowed ladders, the silent and remote rural countryside, sleepy villages, violent unrest, a street collection, tin cans rattling with coins, poets insanely connected to the membrane of humanity. This is the end of modern civilisation (as we know it). What is waiting to meet racing us on the horizon if not immortality, the point of hellish terrain meeting eternity closing in on us cleverly and with speed?

Life is different for

Lovers of poetry, they see that

'Poetic' energy everywhere

They go in the wounded, in ritual

In nature, the veiled psychological

The surface of the silence is a

Sure fire of intelligence like

The dissolve of the seasons

As it moves from unity to one

Redolent picture to the next

Determined to change because

It is in their nature like a fisherman's

Thievery of the flapping soul of the

Fish in its belly

Life is different for poets

Caution is anathema to them

If the poet says the bay is moonlit

Or a man has a wife made of stone

Or that there is healing in the

Elementary, mercy in a Black River,

Then his dream is his truth

Animals have always beguiled

The poet, to feel inspired is not

Enough there is always the road

Like the all-consuming view of the

Sun as remote to me as sea glass

That is the miracle of the poet

How intimate he is with nature

Its singing perfumed machinery

And the estate of the moon

Illuminated bold loveliness

Breathing down my neck–its light

Buried in my hair along with

The flag of stars–potent waves

Steeped in the history of riverbeds.

I wished someone could have told me in my youth not to doubt in my heart and that what I am writing about now is made up of something pure and everlasting. Even though we can never predict what is going to happen in the future, that knowing of all-knowing rogue subterfuge. I mustn't become complacent in my faith and neither should you. I'm walking too. We're accomplices walking that road, master and apprentice, teacher and learner, reader of a writer's notes and a writer making notes. Mother's milk across nations is the milk of human kindness but not in my house. My mum is a wretched kind of woman, emotionally unstable with the mood swings of an alcoholic in search of their next buzz. She's sprouting snakes from her head and I'm transported to childhood. She's made me hate her again. I've grown to love that hate. Her womb fashioned me. Perhaps in a perfect world, I would have been freer.

You are the song I love to sing

Goddess-mother, as you illuminate

The world around you I am illuminated.

She moves me like the force of natural disasters, abandons me with the gaiety of a child and buries her swan-neck in the sand when I am on the verge of tears, inconsolable or a breakdown. I think she knows what she does. Pain feels like an iceberg, separation anxiety, a disorder psychological in origin or a deadline rising up to meet me. There was a phase in my life, a period that has thankfully passed now when just watching my beloved satisfied me. I could feel the dance of time, its motion spinning through me, spinning through the air every time he looked at me. But I am not an affected girl anymore reading romance novels. The art and the game of mindless devotion no longer move me, that and the gulf of passionate and warm embraces no longer closing in on a blue shirt and me. It makes me ill to think of that place in time. Beloveds' have given way to books and research, more of a rigorous academic lifestyle. It suits me.

Missing you listening to the river

Could you be dead in the arms of angels?

A hallucination in a gang the Salvation Army

Can you see me? Look, I am vanishing. I am vanishing like the Cheshire Cat in Wonderland. A hiss and I melt like ice cubes in a glass. The house is crowded what with all the live people and the ghosts. Wounded, I poisoned my body with food, eating everything in sight until it was over and only scraps, gravy, mashed potato were left on the plate. I tried to fight against it but I couldn't. Self-pity and worthlessness reigned supreme. My late grandfather was mute on most issues. I seemed to have inherited that part of his personality. Discontent is evil and its bad cop good cop twin, spirit, makes me feel. In this house, we sleep to dream and not the other way around. I do not have my mother's tennis legs. I have not inherited her features. No, I look like my father. My hair is a bird's nest. I have failed miserably because I am not lovely. I do not sit still. I am not quiet. I do not speak only when I am spoken to. I am an egoist, my brother says. 'Catherine you must stop being an egoist.' How can I stop when I don't even know what that means when I don't even reach for it, when I don't even bother?

I gave away something I treasured

Something personal – a book of poems

Filled with dreaming and secrets

That I have breathed into life on

Blue lines, thin, cold, pale pages

Perhaps if my first memory of childhood were wading into a river searching for symmetry amongst the pebbles I wouldn't have pushed the red self-destruct button. If I hadn't waited for that beautiful winter woman of a mother to speak I wouldn't have met and cradled darkness halfway down the night sky, with a field of stars in magnificent and otherworldly bloom. What if I had carried a painted moon in my hands and the sun in my pocket? (What if God were the sun in my eyes? What if I could fathom out the blue skies, skipped on the cement in my backyard, played hopscotch, stature and Simon Says? What if I had experienced all of that as a child instead of the family drama? Is this what my mother wanted for her children, for them to rage against her, bully her, curse her out, wear her nerves thin and try and control her because those were the lessons that she had in turn taught them? We might have soft hearts but we can cut you like a knife, deceive and manipulate and hate. Let's not forget that most negative of all negative words.

You betray nothing say nothing

It wasn't as if I did not care for you

Or love you was indifferent to

Your feelings your serious intent

I wasn't ready for the major

Responsibility for the blood to boil

Inside my veins for your embrace that

I've never forgotten the rush of

Blood to my head you did not come

With signs, instructions and labels

This is what you left me with

Heavy with light like the whirling

Brightness of stars I called your home

Your country a black hole of vertigo

Love was a ghost inside my head

My sister has returned to Johannesburg. The house is quiet. It is late afternoon. I must cook. It is a sensible kind of thing to do because when the house comes alive then everyone will be hungry. And so the minced meat is cooking, boiling in water in its own oils and juices. The pot is simmering away. I still have to watch it though. I sniff the air. The kitchen smells like the inside of a butcher. Blood, animal guts, skin, entrails and raw. It's no fun preparing food and then eating for one, freezing the leftovers, eating out of the pan with a spoon instead of a fork in your pyjamas. But who is going to see that anyway? Who is going to tell on me?

You come to

Me now in a dream

Of wildflowers in

Summer rain's open

Spaces leaving its

Imprint on ancient

Wet leaves

It's the first week of the New Year and my sister arrived brown and healthy looking from Thailand. I note disapproval in her eyes. She looks me over as she steps into the house. She's beautiful, much like my mother, so much like her in mood and behaviour. Sometimes she scares me half to death. She has brought me a T-shirt that says, 'I love Phuket'. Instead of the word 'love' there's a big red heart. She stayed for ten days spreading her money around, buying golf shirts, socks and vests for my father, picking up the book by Simone de Beauvoir that I ordered at Fogarty's without question. She went shopping with my mother. The two of them joined at the hip, leaving me out of their bubbly conversation, ignoring me as if I didn't have a clue. She didn't say it. She didn't have to. I know what my sister is thinking.

Turning as dark

As the other side of

Humanity, a volcano

Woman feasting

Upon the alien subterfuge

Of the roughness of the galaxy

That is how I imagine you

Her mood tasted like medicine, Lithium, Zyprexa, a bitter pill to swallow. She is thinking, 'Look how normal I am compared to you. Fast-forward to the future. I am a self-righteous, bright and independent working girl. I will not have a replay of my formative years in slow motion. I have forgiven, moved on, pushed everything to the side that is most alarming in quiet, meditative thought, everything that is past has gone into history. I am not about to unpack that again. I am living this perfect life and you are not. You're nearly middle aged. You can't change now, Catherine. It is too late.'

I don't have anything to circumvent that mendacity. I feel empty inside, a little lost. She has that effect on me and so do images of hard, sophisticated and successful women. Why do I want to escape? I want to say, 'Look at me.' I want to scream but that would be a crime. Ladies do not scream.

I can feel the sea in

My fingers mixed with

Salt, sand and light–

The roof of the virgin sky its

Beauty burning bright-blue

Overhead there are two pairs

Of eyes here yours and mine

Ladies wear lipstick, hats, they go to church, speak in hushed tones, blush and they don't use words like 'sex', 'sexual', 'feminist' or 'queer'. What they do not do is become advocates in their community on the awareness of social issues.

Sly drenched skin empty cold spasm

Proof of finding the headline problematic brutal

In my head always in my head

Once I did find love, a sweetness, someone compatible, older and experienced. Ah, it was outside of the home, the dysfunction, the anger and it numbed me. Those seeds were sown but that is a scene from the past. It burned my heart, fired me up from the inside and threaded the bare minimum from my intellect to connect with the pulse of life and all things that were opposite to my creativity, all things that were opposite to and represented by my mum. If life can be cruel then falling in love is even crueller. You never choose whom you're going to fall in love with, the environment and the circumstances you find yourself in when it does happen. All that jazz is not just jazz. It is like hitting your head against a glass ceiling or a brick wall. It hurts. I talk about love here because this is the only way I can express my love for my mother through talk, my journal entries and stories.

How much

It takes to love you—

A divine you, with

My head a bird's nest,

My heart a scar

And the image of this

In my imagination.

For all of my life in front of me lay the world and it appeared to me to be a stage. To succeed all I had to do was act and everything that I wanted came to me except my mum. I was a pilgrim but travelling lost its shine over time. The more years that went by, the more I wanted to stay in one place, grounded, stable. If I was anxious as a child I didn't show it. I was fearless, a toughie.

And their reality

Is revealed in the icy grip

Of the winter rain—cold

And wet demonstrating

That time is an earthly thing,

A meditation of sorts.

You strike me like a blade.

Look at me now. I'm vanishing.

The sky has turned black and there's no turning back.

The Drowning Visitor

As I write this letter to you it is a lazy kind of predestined Sunday morning. I am burning here. There's sun, a breeze and the streets are deserted but the voice of a minister carries from down the road right into the house where I am sitting. You're probably thinking why am I not there with the rest of them, believers? I am with them in spirit. Why am I not praising and worshipping? By now you must know how I feel, that the church is political and the church leaders have no sense of feeling or empathy for the masses. I have seen how some men will fight for positions for power and status. I find it unpleasant.

There are birthdays, weddings and christenings to celebrate that I will never be a part of. I am making peace with that. Then I come to talk of marriage. Marriage is so special, that act, kingdom, that sacred union between two souls, the commitment, the sensual, familial blessing at first in disguise.

Perhaps it isn't meant for me (I am not the kind of daughter of the marrying kind). I want to be and live in a world where I'll be strong without the speeded-up race too, falling into the net of and the curse of materialism, material things. You showed me a world (the point of origin being metaphysics and esotericism) I could finally undertake to understand on my terms.

So tell me the secrets of your heart where you take colourful refuge like the image of a beautiful crystal shining in the sun. If there is nothing ventured then there is nothing to be gained so always venture into and with the occasional and fragile and the anticipatory element. Aren't we all paralysed by the tension of solitude? What is an extraordinary masterpiece if not the creative impulse bonded to sorrow and suffering? It is lovely to be happy but it is never quite enough. But it is in those quiet, feverish most delicate moments where all the difficulties of solitude reveal the veil of stigma. So we are condemned to exchange pleasantries and the spirit of the unclean and decay, imprisoned, locked into a crossing, building bridges, the familiar, the communion of humanity with nature and the connection with life. Has the paradise of heaven forsaken me as I write this epiphany?

I am happy to report nonetheless that life presently is beautiful and it is a journey that must be embraced. To exist, as I write this to you, I am at pains to say that I have met up with the dangerous and cruel world. I have seen what the dark side, its black underbelly has to offer and I have come to no harm. I am older, wiser, more self-aware, less caring about what other men and women and children (strangers really) would think of me and say. And if they would laugh at me even I, I think I would try and see the humour in the situation now. My senses now have unlimited powers. And I think I have God to thank for that, not the church which is, as I have already said, so political in their outlook and movement amongst the community where I live and who damn people at a moment's notice. There are times that I will also not speak of to anyone. My humiliations, rage, that furious, hypnotic anger that rendered me limp.

So limp like a rag doll I have put up walls and I have convinced myself, willed myself not to write about it but it comes through though via the force of the goals of my lucid dreaming, my habit and the culture and the nature of my subconscious.

Is there nothing that can alleviate the pain and curtail the presence of those shadows or the void of an Outsider or am I predisposed to falter into the darkness, that mirror image of hell? Draw nearer to your dreams because they will release you from the prison of the torture of mundane life. And when you write, do not think that it is not an authentic part of you because when you write, the divine is present in the familiar, in the supernatural, the natural and of course it goes without saying nature. The latter must be included here. The good, the brilliant, the immortal will come. First things first. In the meantime, you must be creative. You must experience loss and passion, the ego and the fragile when you are at your most vulnerable. There is even poetry in poverty, even in materialism (and here I am talking about the poverty of the mind). Use every scrap of your life experiences because they are rich. Have admiration.

It is a useful tool/instrument. Never forget where you have come from. Respond to that all-seeing.

Never forget the people who love, support, motivate and think that you are brilliant, a savant and a genius. Don't fool yourself thinking that they are not out there because they are, they are- you just have to know where to look. And don't forget those who hate, despise and hurt you because all intention will transform the internal, introspective you. Never stop telling yourself, 'Send this to a journal' because how will you ever become great, more knowledgeable, a writer held in great esteem, change modern society's immoral norms and values if you fail to try. And that emptiness, desolate-kind-of-spirit-drowning-in-loneliness that comes over you, corners you at a moment's notice at the end of the day, and that serves to annihilate the writing process, any progress you have made, it is the most natural feeling in the world for any would-be poet or writer.

Do you agree or are you hesitant that all of writing and writing poetry is a way of life? A ghost can give you security but then again not all ghosts are harmless. They can live and breathe inside of you like an amoebic organism or something organic like the aberration of mental illness, something with a queerly psychological bent or something to do with biology. It is very simple. I am writing to you, always to you. I am trying to solve all of life's iniquities while I still have it in me and while I still have the time. I am trying to console myself crying out for justice. A writer sees

65

the beauty in illness, in a birthmark, everywhere they go and it makes a permanent mark on them. It is written in a subtle code that only he or she can understand, permute, and take cognizance of.

But you are cleverer than wish fulfillment and the past ghosts inside your brain are. Feeling shy is a disease and there is nothing brave, or worthy or beautiful about it. It is a feeling, that sense of shame that all poets and writers must let go of and surrender if they are to move on to the next phase of their occupation. Your stellar viewpoints always arrest me and make me think that perhaps as a female voice I can write about the wild rural countryside in the southernmost part of Africa and the poor, despondent inhabitants looking for a way out of their environment's circumstances and never finding one. Or I could present the lives of the dispirited, unmotivated youth, the unemployed, the questions of race and of faith, the bewildered, the wretched, the crippled, tales and talk of ancestral worship, circumcision, rites of passage that the media misrepresents.

Media has no livelihood to respect or to be loyal towards the downtrodden black masses. Friend, who has both sound morals and values and who is a believer, spirit-sister, what do you think, what consumes you to distraction? I reckon they have to sell airtime to advertisers and their journalists have to win major international awards. It is silly of me to think the world would think like I do and be sympathetic, hand out food parcels or start a soup kitchen, have a jumble sale with old clothing that has the scent of years and people sticking to every thread of them. How silly of me to think that other people would be inclined to feed the hungry and clothe the poor. It is the wish of a child and I am a woman, although a concerned child-woman in some ways drowning in waves of despair. I am tired of 'drowning' but it has helped my poetic development. I must be thankful for that and my sanity.

Relaying and documenting truth should be the function of newspapers and live television but for the most part, it isn't. Ah, to have the energy, flow, the play, limbs and the insight of a child once again. Seeing sense in the aftermath of being coddled, the ripple effects of permanent midnight and abnormalities coursing through their childhood long after. And so what if childhood is continued into youth and into an adult's realm? At first, the perception in saying that youth is wasted on the young is not a reality until you focus more and more on your own vivid experiences of life. Living with hunger, disease, cancer, diabetes is tragic, that and abject poverty. Don't we regard loneliness, illness, being disabled in some way, the despair unemployment, domestic violence, rape and alcoholism brings to the heart as being isolated incidents in society when it shouldn't be regarded in that way at all.

Perhaps we're really all cowards under the cover of Apocrypha (sham).

As I write these words to you, friend, I do not think that there is anything elegant about illness although it has taken to me like someone who is deathly afraid of vertigo. Your words in return move my spirit.

Send this to a journal, my mind says and I become excited, gleeful like a child who is eating a plum filled with sugary sweetness. When images like that spring to mind, then I think to myself my childhood and the past with all its helpless regret that I sometimes lose myself in. It can't have been all that bad and what is 'normal' anyway.

There are always four possibilities within reach for any writer. I would like to share this with you if I may. Life, death, feeding the beasts and feeding ghosts. The fifth one is much like the senses, that the flow of poetic motion always needs an ending. When I was young, a child on the brink of puberty, my brother and I shared the same kind of rage. We would cling to the sounds of imagination, the disc of the sky in our environment and when it hurt too much we would do what instinct told us to do. String our closeted maturity, culture and our 'secret annexe' and art together and put thought and pen to paper in a diary. The sweet face of the world was our oyster. It was our empire. It was our secret. I have those notebooks still. A4, black, bound, thick exercise books meant for learners filled with scrawled scribbling. We lifted each other up with our own velocity and inherited each other's childhood before we blacked out and hit adulthood running.

Scared to death to 'run away from home' and scared to run towards the future.

The tiredness that comes with ill health remains a bother.

I have convinced myself that history only keeps repeating itself if you, if society if a nation and if the being inherent within all of us gives it permission. The being that believes that there is healing multiplied in name, identity and your own personal space in the world and peace of mind. It is only presidents and the president's men who ordain war. A mother will never send her sons and daughters to war if she realises the realities thereof and what of the realities of my war, that battle of battles. The battle with the opposite sex, with females my own age who do not see anything that I do as remotely feminine, my mother breathing down my neck. Why do feelings of friendship, the ache that will not subside, love and passions seem to be what other people have? I've become aloof and indifferent because the circumstances I have allowed myself to find myself in have swayed me from the positive to a negative light.

I had a visitor today. She tried to push her way past me to see if my mother was in the room (as if my mother would be hiding away in the bedroom, my room, my sanctuary). She paid no attention to me saying that mummy is resting. 'Is she sick?' the stranger asked. If she wanted to go from room to room, I would have allowed her to do that. She was being obstinate. I know what a woman like that thinks of a woman like me. I have not fulfilled my duties as a wife and a mother. I am past the childbearing stage. I have stagnated while my ideas have rested in wondrous flight and whose fault is the former. It is certain that I do not carry that blame alone.

Burning in the Rain

It is too cold to swim but she takes his hand. It is beach weather but it is still too cold to swim. She knows she is being brave at this point; even her rage is poetic as she feels the world, her world and the information in it blackening around her. Everything is becoming more and more intense (she can feel it in a jarring physical sense in her cells), barbarian, savage as she clings to him, her life partner and most of all she also feels mindful of detaching herself in secret from him. She is waiting for him, never questioning or fussing. Waiting for him to join her where she is outstretched on her side, her side of the towel and she is smiling up at him.

'Here, let me dry your hair for you.'

In the car, he pulled her hair and before she could even blink back the tears he slapped her hard in the face.

Curls never smelled as sweet like this before. It's the sun. The sun pressed against her cheek. Her body is brown and tingling all over from the swim and the wind and her tears. He's an invincible work-in-progress. In the interim she's left to burn, to explode. The lines are there of her passion, her experiments into family life (cohabitation), intelligence and her value to this the most modern of societies. Her survival she thinks up to this point has been extraordinary.

'Hold still. Hold still. There's sand in your hair.'

'Pull yourself together right now or else I'm leaving you here.' She licks her lips and tastes blood. Has it stained her clothes, she wonders? Blood is hard to get out.

Dianne in the kitchen, out the door, walking, in the afternoon quietly laying down in the bedroom with the curtains drawn, frying steak or chops, watching the hiss of chips in the pan for his lunch (instead he comes home with pizza, a weak smile on his face and he runs his hands up her arms, up and down her back until she feels light governing all her movements), watching the daylight until it is gone, listening to the forked tongues of laughter coming from the television. She feels all of it sliding through her as if she was a string on an instrument. It smells like rain so she gets up and stands in the draft, closing her eyes. The door is open. The security gate locked and bolted. Is it to keep her in or the madman out? She believes in him and whose fault is that. Who's to blame? Has she gone mad?

Is he finally going to kill her? This scene has not lost its touch and the only thing that is going to take the edge off of things is if she starts to scream.

The next day the phone rings. It's her sister, the one from Port Elizabeth, the younger one, and the outsider of the family. 'Is he ready to start a family yet?' is usually what the hot topic of discussion is, not that why are you crying? What happened last night? Talk to me? Why do you let him do that to you?'

If she checks in the bathroom mirror, will he notice the turn of her head from the bed? She is drowning, Dianne is drowning but can he see?

The words coming out of her are, from the darkness of her tongue, are broken links in a chain. There is no inner space, no room for forgetting the violence. When she is done with the out of town call, she plates two portions of biryani for herself, which the other sister, the eldest out of the four of them, the matriarch made for the entire family. When Dianne has

71

had enough of feeling wretched, she sits on the couch and eats in front of the television before he comes home from work in the evening. He only comes home when it's dark out. God knows what he gets up to or with whom, she imagines to herself. She has exiled herself from the hive of shouting, the flying fists when he has her pinned to the floor under his weight, when she has blacked out.

'Have you gone insane? I've had enough. I'm going to leave you.'

'Have you really had enough, Dianne?'

'It's all a fog.' She told the magistrate. She knew he didn't believe her but she said it again as if he had misinterpreted her the first time. 'It's all a fog.' The magistrate had seen this kind of case before. 'I can't remember. I don't know the exact date. I did not call anyone. No, I didn't pick up the phone to call the police or a trustworthy family member whom I could confide in.' She didn't add that she couldn't move because she was in so much pain and her jaw hurt and she thought he might have broken one of her fingers. She didn't add that he; her boyfriend had sent dishes with the leftovers of their half-eaten supper crashing to the floor. She remembered how dark his eyes turned at the table at the mention of his mother calling earlier that day when he was not at home.

'What did you say?'

'I said nothing. I just said that you would call her back as soon as you got home.'

For Dianne, she finds nothing to wound her imagination, that illusion of all illusions without flaws that delights a child and even more so, a woman, a female poet waiting in the wings. So when she says those words, 'I believe in you' or 'I love you', she says it in part with fear, as if some harm will come to her if she does not say those words with meaning and a giddy, mad dance of happiness, as if she is standing on the brink of a new

72

world that beckons.) Her alienated family remains alienated, everything in her world that she can no longer cope with becomes more or less challenging to face. She begins to fear voyeurs, walking around with her life history inside their heads and then there's she, ever so willing to give it up at a moment's notice without any hesitation at all into her work.

'I didn't touch you that time. There's not a mark on you. It's just shock and panic rushing through you. That's why you're trembling. I didn't mean to scare you like that.'

Hours pass. 'What is wrong with me,' Dianne asked herself with the bedspread under her chin. It's afternoon and she is still in her robe. 'What has finally defeated me, all of that anger bottled up, fizzing inside of me? Was it the holocaust in childhood that exploded in my face like the freezing cold in winter, while I played in the dirt, played at 'being mother' or was it the veteran inside of me's damage, rage and brutality, the poet's inside-out abnormal sensitivity, the black dog of depression, that coveted prize of recovery that followed spells of mental illness that came with youth.' She is tired of being brave, her suffering in silence and inclement rage. There is no heady, formidable sky to reach out to her in her physical pain and offer her solace. She is not perfect.

They are not perfect people. He says, it was just an accident waiting to happen and that she is just a voice with no sensation of armor.

She is the firm catalyst and when he starts swinging wildly at her, he cuts her deep to the very heart of her until she feels she is nothing, not worthy of being spoken up for, just a heap that has bottomed out that once had the potential to be buoyant. Cry baby standing her ground against brutality, a fragile bird caught in the fray of domestic violence, hair unkempt and one emotional cripple tied in chains to another; she finds her own blood enthralling. He wipes the floor with mummified her. She is stained by darkness that flows out of his fighting spirit to the point where her dreams meet reality; she is just a passenger. She only comes to life in silence, when she realizes what her situation is.

All she can do is shout out loud. If she quivers at the sound of his voice, he will leave her like that, watching her soul spill into the ether.

What does she need a social worker with a rapidly increasing in-tray of case studies for? It's not like they're considering marriage. These skirmishes are just skirmishes, intermittent but she can still blot them out. She drifts in and out of waves of real-time, paralyzed by periods of resting, imaginatively counting the seconds between the blows before finally falling asleep. She feels as if she belongs to a tribe of moon-women. Everything about them delicate (suicidal) and if physical harm should come to them (if they walked into a door for instance) they would go to the moon hospital surrounded by caring nursing staff, head doctors who are experts in their field. He cares. He does. Why would he apologize, buy her expensive gifts?

She can't go out, not like this and she has told him this but he's not listening, doesn't give a damn or he's not paying attention. 'Use makeup. Hurry up. We're going to be late.'

There was still something inside her that wanted him to stay. She was frightened of leaving, what that kind of ultimatum would say to her sisters and brother. She would be set loose on the city as a single again. She was too old for that scene. Through all the uncertainties holding her back and the silent treatments she endured in front of the television, in the bedroom, from the bitterness choking her, that climbed into her, curled up inside of her, head spinning she ran water for a bath adding bath oil under the hot water tap. She watched the water turn a constellation of milky white. She was a kept woman, the proverbial housewife with spiritual and physical tasks demanding her attention with nothing to fill up her time but to look after him and his needs.

Being emotionally dead was a serious condition. She needed to replenish the energy she was at a loss to explain how it got away from her. 'I can break you.'

She knew that her dependency on him had to be seen as an addiction, 'Dianne's' addiction. She slid into the hot water, a rag doll, her features out of focus in the mirror, far away from her conscious being. She closed her eyes as if to brace herself from a fall. To reach the green fields, the other side of the mountain, you had to climb hills. All of life is drama and drama is a painful way of learning, Dianne and you are slowly becoming a master at that. Even when he wasn't there in the house with her, she could hear him breathing down her neck, stalking her as if she was prey, carrion, talking to her as if she blind. It was too late for her to learn how to look after herself. She had to be joined to another soul to feel strangely creative. That was part of her generation's Lifestyle.

'I can't be held responsible for your behavior, Dianne. You're behaving like a child, talking like one, acting like one. Does that make you feel brave, standing up to me?'

Tea, a private affair for her, always helped to put everything away, to shut the face of her depression up as far as humanly possible. In a time-capsule, it had more perspective. She could let go of the song of the wind in her hair and him trailing markers of black lines wherever he went and beneath the highs of that surface laid alarm, still waters and the intertwined remains of a girl. She would leave the bag in a mug, pour boiling water over the teabag and leave it for a few minutes. For her 'going out, flying away' face she would stand in the bathroom curling her eyelashes making Hollywood-lashes, applying lipstick, rouge, scent and powder but for now she relaxed and opened the hot water tap again.

So, she would continue to feel like a foreigner in their home (it was her home too, after all, she was the one who kept the home fires burning), struggle against his fury even if it was futile. She packed away the empty bottles of wine where he would not find them and every evening she would compose herself before he came home. If she conceived, the child would be demanding but her splintered life would come full circle. The spiritual quest that had spread for most of her life in front of her would come to an end, normality would reign. But would that be enough? She remembered the day at the beach, waves crashing over her head, bluish sky, while inside she felt miserable, homeless while the commodity of the sun burned up, leaving her a luminous falling angel.

Under World

Of the brutality of my illness 'Iris' is left in the corner. Love me up. Fill the void. Nothing, nothing ever seems to.

Iris the poet

I'm a formidable workwoman, workhorse by nature and an experimenter of sorts. Isn't every poet? I am also deeply moved by art, I have a passion for work, I am attracted to the vital energy of love, death and consciousness, God and movements, observations, spirituality. I hope to speak about life in my poetry, about how it anchors me when I need to be, when my thoughts need to be reigned in and anchored and how it frees me in another sense, another world. This world that I reach out to, speak about and come into contact with is the world that finds itself in communities. Here neighbourhoods occur of parallel dimensions of the meditative union, of feeling the nature of a supreme being, of the whole of familial love, the drama, greatness of life in poetry and how it is acknowledged, the dream sequence of dream sequences in words. I celebrate the private self of the Outsider in verse, the loneliness the Outsider feels, the blank pressure, the threshold, and the inclinations.

Iris again

I often feel outside of myself in crowds, sitting in the car in traffic or even when I am by myself with the still, small voice, that internal monologue as if I am having an out of body experience without my permission. But I firmly believed that it came with the territory. Poets must suffer, must brave the storms of tragedy, must deal with the blows life deals them, and must learn to be, jive and jest. They must learn to amuse themselves on their own. Poets are roses wrapped (trapped) in glass vases. What do you do in an empty space except to expect the complex, paint it in diverse colours and patterns? How do you go about organising it into a meaningful whole? Look, even my scars from childhood, youth, the country, and the personal attack of city-life are pure and the waste of the elegant wasteland inside my head. Even though I have a constant craving to put away the sun in a rain cloud of rage.

Iris flowering after sickness and a funeral

The tall grass was like moving pictures amongst the glowing ochre. It's written on us, isn't it? I can feel the solitude in a leaf, when trees whisper to each other, in the afterglow of twilight, that warm and balmy haze speaks to me, all the summer in it. I've lost all of them now that she has passed on. There's a disconnection on the telephone with all of them. I have nothing to say to any of them. My aunt is dust now or an angel, stimulus or an impulse, a thought or living in a dream world and I have been left on my own to flower, to adventure into the greatness of the unknown, its brutal and aggressive nature. I know something of those tokens. I must remain vigilant of the occurrence of mania; the mass of contradictions that arises with euphoric highs that explodes into life behind my eyes. It hustles me swiftly from stillness to the multiplicity of madness. I didn't say goodbye properly. I didn't cry.

Iris (wishing that her sister would speak to her) and Gracie on the telephone

'We need the money. I'm just asking because we need it.'

'I don't know what you want me to say.'

'Okay Gracie (but I am just trying to sum it up the best way I know how). Thank you for listening anyway.'

'Okay then. Bye.'

'Goodbye (why do you have to be so cruel).'

The measurement problem

'Daddy, I told myself I wouldn't telephone her.'

'But you did.'

'I know but it was a mistake. Mummy's side of the family, they're all toxic for me. The being of the stigma of all mental illness is toxic. I don't want to have anything to do with them and that's my final say. Say I won't telephone her again. Please, just say it daddy. Help me.'

Welcome to Iraq

'You can work.'

'So, you're saying I'm lazy.'

'Bipolar hasn't stopped other people.'

'Who are these 'other people'? You mean people who come from money, who were raised to be good citizens? What do (the bloody hell dammit I am not a child you're talking over) you mean exactly by those words?'

Adam's Wish for his daughter Iris

'If you say you won't Iris then you won't. It's as simple as that. What more do you want me to say?'

'It's as if Gracie is saying bipolar is my self-inflicting wound. As if I asked for it, that it's my fault. Of course, I'm not expecting her to take responsibility to live my life for me. People don't change. Materialism is important to her. Lip-gloss is her god. How can I have a conversation with someone that I have nothing in common with?'

Catching ghosts by putting bags over their heads

In those days nobody spoke of mental illness. It's not as if people are talking about it now. They're writing about it, the wreck of its torment, its oppressive gestures and perhaps the physicality of it but it is still spoken in a hush. It is driven with hands and clenched fists behind closed doors into a private realm. There are no shortcuts when it comes to dealing with ghosts. You have to face them high, head on and with your chin up.

The invisible interpretation of inventing Sylvia

For all her life Gracie treated her sister's as if she was a walking-taking-productive-functioning-disease. She was a cold and disenchanted pale figure of heat and red dust, scaling the walls of the netherworld of photography underworld and sky. She walked with her Nikon around her neck, a fraudulent poser. If she was pretty or lovely, fair or beautiful she knew it. She would never be my silver lining. She would always let pensive little me burn in her shadow. I have got so much more to live for. My mother's mood is patient. She waits for the perfect moment to despise you, to kill you with a look or to catch you off guard. I believe she is never truly unkind without a purpose in mind. Ah, there is Sylvia, at her most feverish, most high and elevated to her pure height of mother when all her children are present, therein lies her mysterious destruction that is immortalised by its authentic twists, narrow paths.

Aspects of Iris's Mind and Poetry

I will forever hold images of men, the strange memories that I have of them, the things of men as close to my heart as I hold my breath. They have been the ones who have shaped me culturally and otherwise. If it hadn't been for them, their airs, dalliances into a cold and cruel world, their sometimes unforgiving domination, their force of control, their hierarchy, I would not have the peace of mind I have today and that I am committed to keeping at all costs. The weather report, the heat and the rain. That's all we ever seem to talk about. We have nothing to say to each other. I am surrounded by cat-eyed, blood-dripping women that I no longer stalk, no longer wish to have anything to say to. Women who are aunts, daughters, cousins and that most obscene word to me, they are mothers with children who are learning to talk, act, and respond to the world around them like their mothers. God help us all.

Dialogue between two women who are getting older

'Is it hot out there?'

    'Is it raining?'

    'Are the lights out?'

    'How are you?'

    'What did you cook today? Is there a fire burning in the kitchen?'

    'What's the weather like/the traffic like on the roads?'

    'Did you deliver flowers today?'

    'Can I talk to my mother, please?'

    'Just hold on one second. She's in front. What are you guys doing?'

    'We're doing nothing. Nothing as usual.'

    'I know you like to sleep late (its afternoon). Did I wake you?'

Iris and Neil

Shall I write a poem and compare your face to the sun. First on the list of terrifying suspense – Neil held my hand tightly in his. Nostalgia is searching through an album where my funny face is completely unrecognisable. I saw the moon this evening and I was grounded and composed by the stars in the sky. In one afternoon, I was swallowed up whole by a hike. We climbed over rocks, our spirits renewed by the sense of adventure. We washed our hands after our picnic lunch in a cooling stream. Memories are made of this. I wish that you were here with me now. I want to show you this book I found at a second-hand bookstore that I have already reread four times. I wonder if you will feel grieved at the same places I did at the decisions the hard and successful characters made.

Iris on Art

Art mirrors life. Hellish art mirrors hellish life. The gifted (the most gifted at this time in history) youth and young at heart are fighting through the medium of art. Writing is art. Poetry is art. Art is art. To protect our legacy we must make history and end poverty. The higher powers, the powers that be, government, authority figures must push through the segregation issue. We, Africa (our country), the world, we are all crying to be born again. Art can generate a sense and a sensibility of self-worth. With climate change and the wreck of the recession that has hit all of us like a freight train there is a sense of an ending but this also means that there is the familiarity and explicit recognition of a novel beginning. Exposing the self to the magic and the psychological-bent to art constantly, driving its core and the very force that it has as it plays a pivotal, empirical role in society just means that now it is necessary for us to move from consciousness to consciousness like a riverbed drowning in the ocean-sea.

Notes on loneliness. And when I go to sleep it is there and when I wake up it is still there. A half-dream that slips away and all at once it is in reach. I can feel it, I can't see it but I can sense it intuitively. I can't explain why. I can't explain this quantum leap.

Husband and Wife

'Shut Up! Shut up! Shut up! Shut up! Go to the old age home. You're old. You've taken the best out of me and left me with nothing. I won't let you forget that.'

They stared at the ocean as if it could swallow up the tension between them, listened to the din of the waves, ate cold pizza, and drank their warm soda which had lost some of its fizz. She picked the black olives and the pineapple off her crust and gingerly put it in her mouth as if it could cure her fierce depression, the bright, hot zone she was in now. If she was in those waves, she knew that part of her would feel intimidated by the youth that surrounded her. She knew she would still feel the heat of the day, dead in the sea, not just a half-drowning thing, wasted, her spirit slightly disconnected from the earth, her soul frozen stiff, her forehead cool. The sea itself was life. The only things they had in common now were their children. What was love anyway? It had meant separation, a near divorce, awakening to their personal needs, personal space. Did it not mean a happy phase, a shared vision, a power struggle, an aggressive team and gifts on birthdays, anniversaries, family get-togethers, Christmas, Easters?

'You're just like your mother, a liar. You ate your mother's food so don't expect me to cook. If you two are bored watch TV but be quiet and don't put it too loud.'

What had it eventually led to were their marked differences in raising children and the elements of weaknesses in their personalities being pointed out when they least expected it. Jean (not the marrying kind) was the oldest followed by Eve (skating on thin ice in the middle, cute as a button, sensitive, brilliant, traveller, left home for America on a Rotary scholarship where she ended up in Florida going to space camp in high school). Adam was the youngest. Wild, the namesake building walls of armour around him, never given a break from the hell that his parents and Jean, his older sister caused. He was the one who was always caught in the furore, wishing that there was no more reason to have thoughts on having just one more flight from fear, his blood boiling with rage and insecurity. He usually had sleepless nights as his middle sister cried herself to sleep at night, his parents arguing into the early hours of the morning about money, about how much they had and how much they didn't.

'Where were you?'

People break all the time, no lie there and when that wretched break happens something is usually lost, left behind confused or someone is hurt, a member of the family, a child, pure and innocent of the cruel world, dangerous adult men and women. And usually, they need rest, to go on a retreat, be surrounded by a cure like quiet, nature and support, motivation or flowers. Once there were children colouring in books where fragile, sweet, loveable children were cast out like butterflies. A young Jean printing out her name in a reader for her English class, sprinting down the track with a victorious smile on her face on sports day. Eve and Adam reading Jean's novels which were meant for a more mature audience, even older than Jean was when she started to read them. The television would be blaring her mother's soap. Jean, Eve curled up beside her would sit on the floor eating crisps, licking the salty crumbs off their fingers, all of ten (Eve six), lapping the soppy, loving dialogue up.

'I'm going to have a short nap now and if the baby cries don't wake me, call your father. He has to do something around here, make himself useful.'

Jean's mother would call it 'feeling blue', 'daddy is tired, he must rest otherwise he won't be able to work on his doctoral thesis for a few hours tonight'. She would flutter her eyelashes seductively, be lovely, on her best behaviour for a few hours when he came home armed with sweets and suckers for the children and a box of Milk Tray for her. Jean, Eve and Adam would make a beeline for the chocolate treats in the box. The children would eagerly bite into Turkish delight, caramel, peppermint and nuts. And all would be healed. Pots would bang on the stove. A miracle would happen. She would cook, sing hymns that she learned as a child in church, Sunday and primary school. But it would be a front. Calm waters before the storm hit, before the 'ship' (the house, the family) hit 'land' (a flurry of abuse hurled towards child and father, glasses falling to the floor in the passage, chipped, cracked, lying in shards that could draw blood, sheets stripped from beds, dumped in the TV room.

'They're not coming here. This is my house. I don't want them. Take it or leave it, I don't care. They're your friends, not mine. Who's supposed to cook, clean, me?'

How he tolerated her Dr Jekyll Mr. Hyde bizarre, no that was being kind, Jean often thought to herself as a child, growing up, no, her mother's abnormal behaviour, could have tested anyone. Jean was an Outsider, living vicariously through her siblings. She discovered at an early age that she was wired differently than other children at school, her nose in a book, shy and teased mercilessly by her enemies about her hair, her voice (that she sounded 'posh', 'white'), her skinny frame. She found it difficult to make friends. While Adam and Eve happily seemed to fit, say the right things, follow the right path, collect trophies at prizegiving, friends a dime a dozen, study and play hard, achieve, achieve, achieve. Adam delved into comics and his circle. Eve had her own friends. Jean performed poorly academically and on the playground she was too scared to stand up for herself, becoming more and more withdrawn, a shrinking violet as she grew older.

'You're so fat, Jean. If you walk around the block in the evening with your father maybe you'll lose some of that weight and to think that once you had a stick figure.'

It left relatives who were close to the family to wonder what would become of her if she didn't grow a backbone or some willpower. Jean hated the whispering and the blushing at school. She hated ignoring, shrinking back from the stares in assembly or during break when she wandered by herself to the library or hooked onto a group of girls when she grew lonely. She knew they found her tiresome and boring but that feeling was reciprocated. She wasn't really interested in anything they had to say. She couldn't add anything to their brand of humour and conversation, their private jokes about their boyfriends or kissing, their congenial laughter and lively chatter. She knew she didn't look like the other girls in her grade. 'Mature, round, curvy', with their grey skirts hitched up well above their knees, getting all that male attention and all the other girls were much more 'experienced' than she was with the opposite sex. They all seemed to have had dalliances, life experience.

'She doesn't have much of anything, does she Cindy?' She heard somebody, a boy she knew by name only hiss in the line to class.

'Jean's an intellectual. Like father, like daughter. She has to be more positive about herself, work on her inner being. She thinks nobody likes her.'

Her mother snorted hard. When her mother said that to her, Jean didn't feel that there was a light-hearted, playful tone behind it. The wall, the damage, the disaster of a relationship that lay between mother and daughter signalled red, grew brick by brick fast and furiously until she could feel the breath inside of her woven tight into a thread. She replayed her mother's voice inside her head until all that remained of her spirit that she was conscious of, was a glimmer of a stain settling instantly in her consciousness. It wasn't hard for Jean to think that other people; boys and girls her age thought the same thing about her. Eve and Adam were star pupils on the other hand. Both were perfect children, well behaved and on weekend afternoons the three would play quietly together, making their own fun by putting on plays, living in a world of make-believe. Most of it was Jean's make-believe world of drama. She felt she had to protect them somehow from 'hell'. Kisses the one-minute, scorn the next.

'Go to your room. You're being blasphemous. We prayed here. If you won't punish her, I will. Out! Get out of here! The spirit is in this room. We don't want you here.'

Jean began to keep journals as young as eight. When she was older she loved the stream-of- consciousness writing that comes from it, putting staccato-like pencil to paper. Her father was a storyteller (told her stories from the time she was very young as he put her to bed), took her out on long drives over the weekend in the car. They left Eve at home with her mother. He would buy her ice cream in a proper restaurant and read his newspaper while she ate it out of a pretty glass with a long spoon and smile at her as she scraped the bottom of the glass. She purged herself when she wrote. She didn't know how to write about a human being without attaching introspection, pain (pain would dominate with a burning intensity), any physical form of mischief, spirituality, a poet/artist 'burdened' with imagination She slowly and with determination built up, composed the lessons she had been taught since childhood, painting them and ghosts in words and landscapes.

It was the only way she knew how to communicate. Her mother drove her father to the doctor now (the psychiatrist). She sat waiting in the car outside, reading. Afterwards, they would buy something to eat and she would drive to the beach. They would sit in silence, eat, make their way down steps to the sand and take their shoes off, roll up their pants legs and wet their feet. There's something sweet, young and innocent Jean thought to herself when she saw her parents like that. She wished they could be like that all the time. She wished they could have been like that all the time when she was young. Mostly she wished that whenever her mother was mean, cruel or hurtful to her father. Jean liked to think that although her mother won the battle, God would eventually win the war in her household.

Diary, I tell you everything.

Perhaps families are not supposed to be perfect, Jean wrote in her diary. Perhaps the lessons that we learn from the people closest to us are supposed to inspire us to adjust to the world around us as we reach adulthood. How do we learn about the magical crossover between forgiveness and love if not from the relationships that mothers share with their daughters and fathers with their sons? And whether or not that gulf exists, that fragile feeling of loneliness that you remember from childhood, that flame you hope you won't remember when you're grown, everybody feels that way. It is just that nobody talks about it because it's depressing, because it reveals your vulnerable side, perhaps you think that it makes you look like you're weak and sensitive, an ordinary pawn in this cruel, sometimes vindictive game called life. Every family, every father and mother lives with regret, with mistakes they made in the past, the golden opportunities they missed out on in the spirit of youth.

But especially not telling their children enough how much they were loved and wanted, how they were born and created in love. If I ever cried about losing you, Eve, it was because it hurt being away from you, being ignored, being relegated to second, third place. I was not the namesake, the pretty, beautiful, loveable, clever one that had everything coming easy. You not loving me the way I did you, you not worshipping me the way I have done all my life changed me in a negative way. You have lived and achieved your goals and dreams. I have not. I have struggled, struggled to survive, struggled to commit myself to my beliefs (faith and God), to hold onto them when I most needed to, until my spirit became my enemy. You were not there in any shape or form when I spent nights tossing and turning in a hospital bed when I couldn't fall asleep. My reality blurred, twisted and wired weirdly, bizarre until I couldn't tell the real from dream or surreal nightmare.

You were not there.

Never stretches out for an eternity in memory. If I was lost, you were the chosen one on the right path. Never losing track or sight of where you wanted to go, what your destination was, your journey, and your road was an open one. You held the sun in one hand and the moon in the other. I have changed. Not one iota of selfish ambition left within me but you're the same confidant and headstrong being you've always been. The one that was waiting to be let out, waiting for the perfect moment until you left home. You leave your more human side for the ones you are loyal to, the ones you respect, drink and party with, 'the wolves that snap at my heels', 'the healthy specimens'. Their faces hard with laughter, sophistication and higher learning, minus me because you decided long ago that I was not good enough to fit in with your crowd and scene, your country. This is my story. I would like to say, what's yours Eve, but we have never had that kind of close, endearing relationship.

It might not be extraordinary to other people how we have drifted apart over the years. People drift away from each other, apart all the time. There is no law against that. I've missed that relationship, feeling the weight of that brightness like a star. All I see is you, what you've become, what you possess, own, and claim, your kind of superior intelligence, your life inexperience. You, Eve, are not mine. You do not belong to me. You never have and you never will and although for most of my adolescent and young adult life this statement has driven me insane because I couldn't understand what sublime dream couldn't put us together again. You are music and I am dirty noise. You are put-together-perfectly head to toe and I'm living with a fractured heart and the suicidal-hot, schizophrenic mess

91

of mental illness. It is not as if I have waited too long to tell you what is on my mind, what I've fantasised telling you, how much I have loved you, missed you, missed talking to you, confiding in you.

I miss the way you laugh, Eve. Your lovely face, the way you posed for family photographs and copied everything I did, the way you crinkled your nose and slurped your juice as you ran after me with your dolls and your 'blankie'. Your cherished blanket from your crib that covered you when you slept that deep safe dream-sleep of a new-born. But you're not here. You're starting to make a habit out of that. First it was India, Mumbai and now it is Thailand, Phuket. You called on New Year's, landed in January and I and mummy went to fetch you at the airport. But I irritate you, upset and annoy you and work on your nerves. You want your space, creep into bed beside mummy and shut me out, out of sight, out of mind in your outer space. It's not hard to imagine what you're thinking when you look at me. I haven't 'fulfilled my potential', 'lived up to your expectations', so you have learned to anticipate nothing from me, share nothing with me. Perhaps all I have of you is the illusion of you.

We're grown, you said once and the only responsibility we have is to ourselves, to live our own lives. For all my life the illusion of you has been bleeding into my subconscious, my dreams. I've tried to ignore the truth of that and I am no longer quite as confused about it as I once was, but as I grow older it has also grown with meaning. And in the end, the monster is not you but me. But monsters are extraordinarily nightmarish creatures, ghouls with no heart and no soul, flawed and perhaps when you were little, a small girl with a head full of curls living in her already fragile world that is all you saw of me. Mental illness could do that to a person. Strip you to the barest elements, a losing form (truth), extended stays in hospitals with visits from our parents (truth), shapeless pyjamas (truth) and an unkempt, unruly head of dark hair (truth). You were the favourite (fact of the family

92

matters), I never missed that, it was understood and I was the lone black sheep. How quickly children grow but they never forget.

It was the day after Boxing Day. I heard my parents talking, the television in the background, my mother quiet for once and in a relaxed state of mind. My father was eating meat prepared on Christmas day, what was left of the gammon, roast chicken and beef with creamy potato salad, beet stains on his T-shirt, his feet bare, and his belly hanging over his swim shorts. They were both watching the cricket. He scratched himself up on his legs. They were in love once. They shared a first kiss, held hands, held onto each other in the dark at the drive-in, dated, wooed each other, and wrote love letters. My father sent postcards from the continent as he travelled through Europe on holiday from his studies at London University. Now he washes the dishes, cleans his bathroom, sweeps out his bedroom (my parents sleep in separate beds now and after this Christmas Eve they now have separate bedrooms). He mops and dries the tiles. To see my father like this is disconcerting.

Of Adam during his formative years, I remember very little when I look back at 'our lives'. In pictures as a boy he is smiling, pulling a wooden wagon, wearing a cowboy hat, dressed in his Scouts uniform but grown up, receiving his degree he is serious. I don't know in which phase of their lives they were when my brother and sister stopped believing in God, only that He didn't feature as prominently as He once did when we were children in Sunday school and Youth. God simply faded into the background like our toys, into the distant past. And the memories of Sunday roast with pudding and custard. Along with our competitive natures, being a child in the eighties and teenagers in the nineties, going to Model C schools and nurtured in the art of being wholly different from other children your age, bullies on the field and where all sports were taken seriously. Am I too serious, Diary? What else is wrong with me besides stating the obvious, that I am following head-on into my father's footsteps? When my father was sick to death of life and his own was coloured with pale sadness and illness, he too went to the hospital for 'a rest'. My siblings and I played on the thin, grassy part of the garden at the clinic (there wasn't much of it). Under neatly trimmed hedges and trees in Port Elizabeth, we watched our parents cross-legged talking under their breath to each other in hushed tones.

I will never forget those whispers the three of us were not supposed to hear of grownup talk. I (the little, impoverished bird) have improved now that you've gone away, Eve. I no longer trail in your wake wondering what the ending to this drama is going to be like. I can still smell your hair as if it was an elixir. I can feel your child body's magical space where it left its warmth. You could not stop my flight into mania, me bolting into the blackest darkness of the futility of the art of depression and what was at the heart of me. I wanted you to possess all of fragile me, see a picture of the hell that I went through but you wanted no part of that cut-out of the ocean-sea inside my head. Your silence from those years, the year you wrote the Matriculation exam still cuts through me like a knife. My territory has slowly but surely multiplied. Your journey as a goddess has finally ended.

I am a child again. I watch girls wearing swimsuits and bikinis and want to be older, grown up. I watch them as they tease their friends. The ones who seem like they can't swim just put their feet in the water or sunbathe. Girls watching the boys, the boys watch the girls. My mother hisses at me to do something, to stop staring and why on earth did I bring my doll to the beach. I am going to lose her, silly me. I have already lost the safe world that my brother and sister seem to inhabit. I am a nuisance, a pest, despised by the adults around me because I am a know-it-all. If my mother says these things to me, then other people, perhaps even children must also be thinking it. I don't feel anything now. It is becoming easier and easier to feel that way in my mother's presence. I can almost feel my heart in my chest. I don't feel the heat of the day anymore. Instead just a pressure flooding through me that feels like I am on the verge of tears because her words are hurting me. They feel like pins and needles.

I am hurting. The tears don't come. They don't have the guts to anymore. I know that if I fail at that, it will mean the death of me. This is South Africa so we never expected snow. Snow only came in winter, June. Children and even the adults made snowballs and played in it on the news but all I could think about were the poor in the location and shanties. I can feel beads of light behind my eyes. The soft, bewitching, pink mouth that parts in the grotto is not mine and the shiny hair, curls soft to the touch do not belong to me. The young girls and boys that leave hollows behind in the sand this festive season I have nothing in common with, (always, always, always). I remember watching girls as they 'disappeared' with 'nice' boys at the beach as a child and wondered when it would be my turn. Nothing was hot anymore. Not the sand, my bronzed skin, the towel sticky where the ice cream dripped off its stick, the white rays of the sun that seemed to connect with every fibre, cell and fire of my child being.

I remember my mother's floppy hat and how she shielded her eyes keeping her eyes on the waves. People didn't wear sunglasses in those days. All I could think about was how pretty I wasn't. It is only then that I imagine myself in love when I am brought to life by the familiarity of a fantasy life built, stored up extravagantly in words. When I see them as fossils, like bones, that I have to map out; find a location, category and title for everyone. I am immune to the labels, to winter, to the other seasons that come and go with infertility. I am a woman now, growing older and I must learn to endure everything. Beneath my skin my heart beats faster and faster. I have often wondered what the diagnosis is. Perhaps it is both a fear of being found out that I am so desperate to be loved and accepted. The confusion of my childhood played itself out with the older sky above me. Hell down below me where I was a guest treated like royalty because of my mental illness.

The cat was warm, inspiring me to sleep too this afternoon. Sleeping in the middle of the day is a sure sign of depression. I covered my body with the sheet and blankets, rest my head on the cool spot on the pillow but I could only see a dark forest that smelled of dew when I closed my eyes and an outline of a woman who wore a red coat in the moonlight. I could not make out her features, this witch, was she a ghost with her hands covered in blood? Was she a Lady Macbeth spiced up in disguise? An accomplice to something much more sinister, her own death and why was she bleeding? I pulled the covers over my head like a veil. You're dreaming, I told myself. You're watching a frame. I could have screamed. Instead, I kissed her on her cold mouth to comfort the poor thing. She seemed so unfulfilled, lost as I felt. I didn't want her to leave me. She kept me company, gave me the feeling of making me want to live.

Dreams are curious things. It's the nightmares that keep you awake or afraid to fall asleep again. The ocean-sea inside my head tightens itself around me, grips me and its hold feels like metal, a picket fence and a grid. And in the water it attached itself to me with its invisible hooks and I could feel myself flying through the air. I was a good girl again, young and free, holding onto my father's hand, watching him smile at me. In a split second I was grown, a temp in a city with a man who worked across from me who had a beard staring at me. An older man who had a wife, grownup children touching my head, smoothing my hair and telling me how pretty I was and how I didn't even know it. I played dumb staring at his hairline. White hair as white as flowers. And that night they bloomed magically from nothing inside my head like Adam's rib or whalebone. For a moment I was filled with a waving rhythm of shame and then just as swiftly as it had come it was gone like passing gulls.

It was gone like grains on the hollow song of the wind, slipping into a stream filled with rings of the stench of rotting, decaying waste, sinking into a drain where it lost itself in the blue wild, in spells of tides. Where it lingered in brown-golden yellow-red wilderness and then as I flew higher into the rays of air I became a young woman again who was a plaything half-drowning in delirium amongst women who tasted as of things like my mother did. Honey, chocolate, tuna fish sandwiches, all of fish sardines on crackers, salt, the dim, dim candlelight of dinner parties where the grownups drank too much cabernet, ate far too much chicken, potatoes, pudding. I sprayed scent like a saga a little too anxiously, left the porridge burnt at the bottom of the pot that morning; oats. Now I am swimming for my life while my sister in another city reaches for her umbrella next to her front door. I can smell the rosemary chicken but I don't want any feasts.

And so, in the end, we will have to re-consider the truths of life which we were so religiously brought up to believe to be the truths of life and our very existence.

There's a kind of feel-good chemistry in eating and when I've purged all those bubbling molecules inside of me I feel a sense of freedom as if I am the only unique in the world. The pain I feel inside, that I sometimes feel I will harbour forever, that and my mother's voice goes on and on. It connects everything within me, the internal to the external. Outside, there is the glimmer of sanity that I am insanely holding onto but inside I am disconnected from the entire human race, jealous of those who do not have to live the way I do. I have to keep away from people because I am not good for anybody. In rage, when I feel murder racing through me, when I feel the pressure of being manic, blue or darkness visible. I am too good at making you see what you want to see. At least I am good for something. It has been hard my whole life to make that picture seem so

97

perfect. The perfect daughter in the perfect family who was after all not so perfect. There was again only the illusion of what outsiders wanted to see.

The perfect parents who raised children, everything about them flawless except for the one who inherited mental illness from her father's side of the family. So, I dream of ghosts, the weight of water against my limbs, its push and pull, the secret code my mother carries imprinted on her soul. There is only signs of fate, rust, only the fact that someone or thing has been here before me in history. Perhaps it was the dew, state of abstracts and the flecks that mirrored the diamonds in my mother's eyes. Like the wide hollows of eyes marked in cathedrals of stone that left me half-perplexed as a child. A self-portrait of an innocent in this organic of ephemeral societies. Then I know I will be able to flourish viciously. That's the trouble with remembering. You begin to wish.

The Most Perfect Volcano

Most scenarios start with a knife digging into your back, an enemy's face you cannot glimpse, a flame burning bright inside of you when you stare into the distance or think out loud, when a daughter inherits mostly the makeup of her father's genes (this is how this scenario blends into the background of the almost most perfect volcano, which is just another way of putting the weight of mental illness into metaphor, the sword of truth of mania, the wilderness of depression laid bare, to rest in an open field) and a young woman's frightening yet still poetic passage into the annals of men, where she is dominated by men, thrust into their world and trapped by their limitless boundaries.

Their gift to her was her future life as a writer and a poet. It meant freedom and liberated her from the basics of ordinary human life, of being a wife bonding with small children, bundles of energy tightly wound, a husband in tow, broody cousins dispelling the myth of infertility.

She owned these borderline scenarios, mostly with the daily histories of the setting sun and rising moon, journalising in diaries, writing jumbled scribbling but it was the crowds in malls that were the worst of all. With no inner spaces between them, breathing down her neck, emptying the harvest, the countryside of her frail confidence until she felt lost and cold, sadness seeping into her skin, breathing still life into her memory as being a tough, fighting, fearless kind of child. As an adult, she suffered. No golden lightness behind her eyes now. Only fear of the known and unknown, the frontiers of empty space inside her, moving behind her, the potent anguish and anxiety of her mental faculties. It flummoxed her so much so, that she put it to bed with an open heart, an open mind on the flat screen in front of her, straining to recall words, phrases that leapt into existence in her mind's eye and then just as quickly vanished like smoke.

Scenario 1 (hurried notes in a journal)

If I write about myself in the third person it is only because I only trust myself to commit to truths that lie at the edge of what I deem normality. Living a half-life thrust into both madness and despair and in the trailing wake of living a courageous life that is relevant, leaves me both hot and cold, at the thought of being at the mercy of something which I have no control of.

'Be serious.' My tone warned. 'I don't hate you but I don't like what I've become – a kept woman.' (How strange. What did I mean by this when I wrote it?)

I want him to be more serious about me and this relationship (hint). I want to be more confident, less dramatic, less emotional and a little less sensitive when I feel slighted, humiliated and belittled by him, illumined once as a woman caressed in his arms and then a drowning child where water becomes a fleshly thing that refuses to give me up. I don't want to feel like I'm on an eerie collision course every time he hurts my feelings or every time there's some disagreement between us.

If I am a feminist, am I an African feminist or a representative of the world? On reading books by other feminists' struggle and why it is necessary in Africa of all places: We seem to live in a time capsule in Africa where women struggle on a daily basis to become emancipated. Where is this 'revolution from within' Gloria Steinem wrote about and Simone de

Beauvoir's 'The Second Sex' and the woman in Naomi Wolf's 'The Beauty Myth'? Oppressed, abused, illiterate, uneducated, mentally ill, physically disabled (some wear their crutch like an omen); can you sense the tension in the spark of the conscience of a woman from the rural countryside and where is the substance in her 'voice'? It is a cancer of years, a human stain, and just phenomena. It will take the breakthrough of the loud voice of men to fill that void, to lift the female up and put her on her pedestal, call her 'goddess', build a tower of castle wall around her and call it 'self-worth', 'confidence' (he is, the man, who I will call 'Nameless' here, who I am in a relationship with now is not a man worthy of building a castle wall. A bricklayer, a simple labourer takes more conscientious choices in their work than he does).

I am in my late twenties, dumbing down my speech. Today fresh blossoms were crushed in the spray of winter rain; hail rained down like someone was pelting me with rocks. Acid colour spills into the fading sunlight, jerking us back to reality, reminding me of my mother's rage when she had nobody else left to scream at. But she's not here, mouthy, mouthing off at me when no one else is around, yet I can still sense her disapproval.

I've come a long way from boarding school in Swaziland, hiding away. The hours I spent in libraries shaped me, pulled me up and pushed me away from everything that was bad to good. When I'm alone in this flat, staring out my kitchen window through the blinds, living vicariously through passers-by, I imagine somewhere out there's a warm after-glow like angels welcoming a rainbow through a smudged window, reminded of that heinous day as my mother and I are on our way to ICU where my father lays like a child in a pale blue hospital gown; we're late; my mother, a she-devil, races through the traffic to get us there in time.

Thirtysomething. Let it rain, let it pour down, dewy and dreamy, a new halo blurring the images of the traffic, of crowds of people on the streets in front of me while I stand on the edge of this precipice woven into the warmth, the vastness of the design of this emptiness. You are what I need right now, my desire. Bring me closure; finally, to our relationship, bring me back to you.

Scenario 2 (hurried notes in a journal continued)

Lying awake at night thinking of the monster that was you sometimes. Jet black hair, your mouth could be as sharp as razor blades but it could also imprint the rush of wind in the trees overhead in the dimming light, the soughing sound of boats in the harbour in the town where I came from, the whispers in the air of the sea in the dead of night, the history in wet leaves and your handprint on my face that you left me with. You taught me that there were so many futures awaiting me. There were tears while I was trying to change but you stayed the same, incognito, an enigma. It's time to let you go, go to where my faith has gone and surrender you to the arms of another woman, a doting wife and mother to your children, her ceremonial hive of dinner parties, her kitchen, her manor on the hill while I turn to dust in the fire of your eyes. How am I going to learn to forgive?

I'm 17 again, running away from home jaded and cynical, wanting not to feel anything. Everywhere is countryside. Trees are tilted overhead, the leaves are wet and it's a jungle in suburbia, big houses built for family life – Swaziland, it's too green. I can't see straight; my eyes awash with tears or is it just the rain, gluing my lids shut. The hail feels like the cool edge of sea glass hitting at me from all sides, they feel like surreal blocks of ice, stone blocks reminding me I need room to breathe. As if I am in a Dadaist picture, or the picture of Dorian Grey always growing old. I'm ageing as I speak.

17

The sky is a Goodyear blimp just waiting to crash land; bump and grind to a halt. In wet pools, muddy puddles that stick like gum to your shoe, slipstreams of floating junk, dirt, and flotsam in never-ending potholes in roads that are never repaired. We are too depressed to realise the worth of youth when it's gone. It smells like incense burning. I sat on her bed in the hostel after school came out. Lulu braided my hair even though I didn't really like the way she styled my hair, I said I liked it, and she seemed happy with my answer; I didn't want to hurt her feelings – after that we watched the daily soap opera and after it was finished, I said goodbye and years later I didn't know how long that goodbye would last but now I do. I didn't know then I would never see her again in my life, that life was like that, that a life could be filled with white weddings and funerals, christenings and the arrival of death. How it would show up when you least expect it.

I've believed that perfect ending of too many fairytales, read too many books, thought myself clever, pretended that it was going to get better instead of that 'passing through life' feeling, instead of being a casualty I would be transformed into a beautiful, magical being called 'woman'.

Smitten, I have taken to falling in love. It is more of an image in my imagination. The words lend themselves to a song of truth. Saying them brings them to some sought of reality. Smitten, I have taken to falling in love with kindness. It freezes the glitter of my melancholy. I imagine that this relationship I have now will cause dissension and sense with delight the disapproval of the Christian women in my family. Even though a new generation is rising up of women who believe they have a right to sexual freedom, I am not a part of it, that movement.

I learn to give a human face to depression and in all of its naked glory it tastes of a broken vessel, spilt milk and coconut burned black. Hurting I begin to have a perpetual dialogue with perfectionism.

Scenario 3 (hurried notes in a journal continued)

This was the voice of a girl. Port Elizabeth. (Let daddy read over some of the poetry tomorrow.)

This was the voice of a grown woman, much more spiritually aware and emotionally intuitive. When I write, I feel as if God is connecting with me. I feel as if I'm connected to something greater than my self.

I'm 22. In this world, I am more frightened of women, eager to do their bidding, to please them instead of men. Is this psychological, psychosomatic or is this mental aberration organic in origin? My mother has become every woman. Perhaps as a girl, love meant eternal sacrifice to my mother. What did she give up in Johannesburg when she moved down here to Port Elizabeth? Even in adulthood, I can never escape her roots. Of the women I come into close contact with I am left with burning questions. What did 'she' give up I wonder, what has 'she' sacrificed, what is 'her' world like when she leaves this world dominated by office men and goes home, to her own family and children? What are 'her' thoughts? How does 'she' remain absent in the presence of her children and the air that they breathe? If only my father had been more indifferent and aloof to my needs? What would have become of me if he had also rejected me?

Turning in the air, in the middle and then suddenly I'm 32. The depression has roped in a soulful worth of insecurity. It, the depression, is now innate, lodged quite comfortably like a jungle in the city, keenly ominous, still having a dazzling effect from one day to the next while bubbling below the surface of things, flowing within reach, constructed like the passage of mail, a bully in the midst of mall and community life. So the depression figures internally, transforming my existence from recovery to ill health, from shy and withdrawn with a delicate composure seeking powerful walls of comfort, in the presence of strangers, to being as bedridden as an invalid, from the outsider lying in a minefield of discontent dying to belong, to a reclusive poet surrounded by the wonder of nature.

How far is it still to the next hour? Why are there these challenges, scenarios in white and on cold blue lines? I would turn to you and say if you were here with me in this moment, 'Yes, I'm still writing.' But would you care? You never fail to draw a line right through me, surreptitiously bypassing all my internal organs, my pure heart, my imagination, the tomorrow of my gift and I devour it, your attention, in merciful anticipation, you that have no name. Certain words (like your name) still perform with a triumphant inner voice inside of me. It releases me from the bitterness of an old maid, the bondage of silence in this room where sequestered, I write and it takes me to an instrument of peace.

Buried

Good things are born from painful experiences.

Ropes, ropes and more ropes. I have had enough of them, the hangman's noose and their knots with basic tension. I want a pretty city, with bright lights on the promenade as I walk into the sea, as I feel my hair against my skin, my feet bare, the night air so crisp and all I see is the clarity of my mission. The sun has her mistress and there is a man that lives on the moon. I am a drowning visitor. I sink further and further away and I finally grasp the shoreline. Here I am free. I have hours to think, I am no longer trapped by gender equality and who wants to be trapped by equality, brutality, everything gruesome, obituaries, by hours, and things of childhood-making. Starving landscape after starving landscape, brittle like filament, a burst of thirst pulsating like a shiver, a thread of sweat, a breath, a river, shamanic wisdom, the normal who lives next door, the other side of the mirror is buried under smoke, the incessant flap-flapping of the wings of moths, seasons draw wrinkles on my mother and father's face. A green feast shoots up everywhere in the garden and everything seems young, fresh and new again. The rain has its own way of thinking and it is a way that humanity will never understand. It can be a beast. A serious beast with a serious intent who remembers their vowels in a coolly distracted way on a hot-cocktail-drinking day in apartheid South Africa while sunbathing next to a chlorine-blue swimming pool in the backyard. The earth, on the other hand, has a vision of her own.

I see all of these things in the mansions of my imagination. Something is bright within me. I enter into a contract with them. I am lifted up, up and up. I am standing in a forest. I look up and what do I see. The blue jewel of the sky. God's sky. God's forest. I close my eyes, feel the sun against my skin, and imagine standing on the beach, a lone figure watching the waves and their never-ending spiritual love story (spellbinding ghost story) with the shoreline. I step forward feeling the burden, the will of the river-sea rises up to meet me. I no longer stand tall, my wounds are frozen, the physical, the deep pain is numbed and becomes a posture, the world turns upside down and I am being navigated towards something greater than myself, away from painful experiences of the past. The lasagne tastes good. It was made by a prophet, my mother. The prophetess. Once I was skin and bone but they didn't call it anorexia nervosa in those days. In those days I had to 'perk up'. In those days 'I had to pull up my socks', 'put meat on my bones'. These days I think about my ancestors. I have ancestors. Everyone does. Everyone who lives on this side of the world. Dark skin, white skin, mixed race, different faith, rituals and the burning of incense that comes with them, doctrines stored away like a file of a case study in a psychiatric institution (mental hospital) they all tread on religion at some point in their lives. They have their own exact perspective. And when I dream I dream of the waterfall of the past when I was a girl. And everything that I see makes me feel wonderfully calm as if I am made of substance. I remember when I first drank red wine (it came out of a box), when I first tasted basil, felt as free as a bird with a broken wing, drank a soup made entirely out of noodles, fell in love with sushi (fish with no eyes in a blanket of sticky rice), a girl, a boy, the world, a married man who dominated me and the world around me. And so the world of my childhood-making, mummy and daddy evaporated. I still remember the man's skin, his knowledge of the universe, his experience and influence, how his flesh became my flesh, how I could see him as a boy and it was the most beautiful feeling in the world. It made my heart sing. It made words dance maddeningly inside my head, on the page of a book and I could finally see the past, present, future merging into one. I moved from one unpredictable, unusual affair, situation, and relationship to another and I grew up and became more fragile, that is my common sense and sensibilities and my ambitions grew into humility and humility grabbed with greed at the wuthering heights of my pride. The people that I knew once passed on. Nothing unusual about dying, moving to another city, moving forward even if it is towards poverty, marriage, terminal illness, suicidal illness, mental illness, the icy grip of the panic of terror and anxiety. Time. I don't believe in it and I never will. Time steals away your dreams, your soul, your spirit, your childhood. It closes in on you until you are forced to face your deepest fear. Death stands there in the gap from this world to the next. Eternity. It is not loved. It is not nurtured. It is not a paradise-in-waiting.

When I meditate I go inside myself and see God. There is no longer a divide between the wards of hell and the divine paradise of heaven. One is a lake of burning fire, choking smoke and plumes of ash and the other one is locked and a saint stands before the gates leading into heaven. Death has always been there, looking down, or over my shoulder and with each step that I take Death follows me with a steady pace. I've never seen Death's face but I have been frightened that when my time has come my work here on earth has not been done. I do not want to leave anything incomplete. Everything must be put away, packed in boxes, connections that were once as alive as electricity must be disconnected. I've been close to death. Close enough.

I think about you a lot. You were kind, nice, sweet, and younger. You made me feel like a museum piece, a statue. It's been years since I've seen you. Not so long ago we sat and laughed as if we were old friends, good friends. I made you coffee. You made me forget my sadness, my manipulative nature, my family's arrogant manipulative nature and in some small, adequate way I began to feel alive again as if I could survive everything that life had arranged, assembled for me. But I am bad for you.

I am not the chosen one meant for you. How can I make you understand this? I do not belong in your world. There is nothing welcoming or bold about the arrival of me. Choose another. I am giving you your freedom. Hush. Here. Now go. I want to watch you, study you, watch you fail, surrender, let go, fight for the underdog, understand you, comprehend you, what makes you whole, what makes you think, what do you love? What opinions do you have on the current trends in politics, who will you vote for this year, do you believe in magic, why have you not forgotten me, what do you remember, do you have any fears (do you have any fears about my disability), what anchors you? In forgetting you, the pieces, the tiny bits that refuse to evaporate have become distilled beautifully and I also have realised that I need to write more than I need human company. I don't care about ambition.

If other women think you're arrogant let them think that. Don't waste your time, your energy on them. If other men want to destroy you, your empires, your soul then let them think that they are getting away with that. I've forgotten about your mistress, your ego that strokes your vanity (that I can't take away from you). It belongs somewhere else but not in your personal space. Children need the ego. It makes them feel different in a special kind of way in a world filled with ducks and games.

I hate the smell of cigarette smoke but am intrigued by women who do, with their airs and graces, with all their manufactured secrets and that one slim cigarette held between their fingers. The women in my family do not smoke. They're like a union of spies. I only learned about fear late in life. They do not drink red wine out of a box only fruit juice cocktail on special occasions like birthdays, Christmas and Easter. They do not sit for portraits, go to parks, spread out a blanket for a romantic picnic lunch made for two. They only go to the beach in December when it is the summertime in Southern Africa. There's something clean and pure about depression when it is looked at with the round peg that can't fit in the

109

square hole in the eye. Clarity is found and so is rest. The people-traffic-zoo outside is possessed with identity and the idea of not emancipating themselves. Why would they do that if they think that their reality, their dreams, their goals and their imagination is enough for them? The stem grows. The branch reaches forwards and we all move towards the light hoping that it will put the spotlight on us.

When I feel weak inside is when mummy speaks to me. My heart slips and thuds inside of me at the same time. There's no awakened rhythm in that red palace. All the voices of mother, father, mummy, daddy, sister, brother become familiar to me. They are not the same people all of the time and their visions are awesomely vibrant and energetic, burning like phosphorescence, a lone star. They orbit me.

The invisible air tastes like salt. My mouth gulps down slippery seawater that licks the insides of every one of my teeth. I want to feel you inside of me, as I open up to you like the flowers of a manuscript. I've already lost you to another woman. Is she a girl, does she have a matron's figure at a girl's boarding school or is she as dead to you as I am to you now? I don't say these things to get at you, to think as you do, to get inside your head I'm just lost in the silence of violence like George Botha, Richard Rive, Kevin Carter, Dulcie September, Arthur Nortje and when I feel most intensely lost is when I write poetry, that is when everything I've collected in my heart comes out. I really don't care for now's sake if I never saw pictures of you, heard sob stories of you again in my life, your living memory, so romantically-felt is enough for me and it will stay with me until the end of my lifetime.

The heat. It's hot, intolerably-hot and there is nothing I can do to eliminate it. Was I really loved as a child? It serves to improve the lies I keep telling myself. That I am not pretty enough, tall enough, enough for enough's sake. There are millions of children who are not loved, who bathe every day in dust and shit. Life is designed for oppression, ridicule, rejection but also for liberation. In some wanton way the world makes us want to move backwards without us having any say about it.

House torched. It was burned down to the ground with two children in it. The door was locked. The mother was away. There was no father as there is often in these cases. And so another community is brought together but this is no celebration of life. They thought a witch lived there. It shows how fragile we are as humanity. And I am preoccupied with love when the world around me is burning. These are all things we wish that could be buried in peace and dust and memory.

There are happy, healthy babies. Mums that are glowing in blue and white hospital gowns. Their skin radiant with life but what happens when you like writing poetry about death, grief and denial. It is a land that time forgot. This kind of writing (poetry) is writing that so few people can understand. There were no angels on the frontier when pioneers confronted wilderness and poverty in Southern Africa just dust that has been here for millions of years.

The lasagne tastes good. It was made by a prophet, my mother. The prophetess. I've worshipped her all my life. She has taught me how to forgive, how to live, and I am beautifully grown now. Although the universe is still sweeter, purer, more honourable than I am with all its untitled interpretations. How can the extraordinary unconscious of the universe be anything but baffled by humanity? I am. People are not as invincible as they think they are. Freedom fighters every one? Unfortunately, no. Coldness. Aloofness. Indifference. Introspection. Suffering. Water. Ghost nations. Precious bittersweet gifts everyone.

Nothing belongs to us.

On disability

Most of all out of anything in this world I want to become a better poet, a better woman, kinder, a better mother-figure. Odd that I feel maternal. Every day I look at the people around me. Not the people closest to me but the ones I admire a great deal. The world needs people who are kind, women who fall in love, daughters who listen to their mothers, sons who don't end up in rehab, voices.

I picture your voice. The sound of your voice in the world, in your world winter guest. All I have now after thirteen years is the spaces of forgetting, my father, and the pillar of our community. Light, light, the light in your eyes. One day it was there and then again just like that it was gone like a moth in fog, people moving about in traffic caught up in the circus of their lives. I was very much attracted to earning your love like a child was to gaining the unconditional loyalty of a mother. Now all I think about is when relationships come to an end. The humiliation that one party suffers, scorn, rejection but also a great deal of disillusionment in the end. All I see is the cold lines of your anatomy framed by the sun and for years to come you would always be in my mind's eye framed by the sun.

The writer is an artist in the inner sacred cycle, in that space, that land of giants, where even the immortals can be found. The greats like Rilke and Goethe who become immortalised forever by words that are like clay, that foist upon themselves the consistency of clay dry or wet. Plath, Lowell, Woolf, George Eliot. All were writers with their own rituals and their own passages to maturation. They lived in books, guarded, sheltered, protected under a silver lining, a blue sky, green grass. Revenge, hardness, those were

112

things that they carried with them since childhood. It was the atrophied part of their soul. So they reached plateaus. Faces peer at me out of the picture. I don't know them so I pretend I don't see them. Words are like clay. Food was my comfort till the bitter end. It annihilated me around every corner, every turn. When I don't sleep or eat I'm thinking of writing. Sometimes I'm writing gingerly. Sometimes it just comes at me, pours out of me so pure and sometimes it is an agonising waiting game that just kills me to my core.

I write every word down as it comes to mind. Write every single word down as it comes. Don't hesitate. Don't stop to think, to question even if it sounds like a soliloquy.

I'm fourteen again sitting in English class behind Arundhati. We're reading Athol Fugard's Road to Mecca that I've fallen in love with. Arundhati does not eat lunch by herself. She does not sit in the library and do her homework during break times or when her class has a free period. Arundhati is the most beautiful person I have ever seen in my life with wide eyes as wide as saucers. Watery. And hair that is thick, glossy and healthy and black as pitch black as her eyes. Her skin glows. She's clever but not too clever. I know she will go far in the world. I know she will leave her mark one day. I feel a kind of chemistry with Helen of New Bethesda. I can relate with her loneliness, desperation, isolation, her emotional imbalance. Arundhati could never relate to any of those things. She is one of the most popular girls at my school.

When I am twenty-two I meet another Arundhati in the city that never sleeps but seems to wind down at four in the morning. She has legs that go up to here. Who wears kicking boots with stiletto heels and skinny jeans that seem to melt on her svelte skin but who is also insecure, demanding, who throws fierce tantrums in the workplace? I can see by a long way she is going to make her mark on every man and woman in this office space. While Arundhati embraces her winter guest I go-a-hunting for rainbows as

113

ancient as dust and merry-go-rounds of the galloping painted horses' kinds. One day I can't stand him and the next I can't wait to see him torn. Arundhati is his girlfriend. It's another manic Monday. I know she will tell me everything. I know she can't wait to tell me everything. Women just know these things.

I'm fourteen. We're at the gateway to the funhouse. We're standing on burning sea sand, water, ocean waves within reach, the centre of summer, the perfect identity of the nuclear family not yet maverick, reckless, playing at adult games, playing at abandonment and neglect, walking away from responsibility, birthing a symphony of harmonic values. But there's a sadness to the day. A kind of poverty as if we've lost our shot at the big time, social cohesion or lost something never to be found again.

And so we forget that the sun is in our eyes and we all blink madly at our tears but we're mad with joy. We're one big happy family just like in photographs, or in television programmes or films. Mother, daddy, younger brother, sisters. Look. We're getting laughs. It's effortless. A kind of easy living. This living is the best kind of life.

And so, we forget the sun.

Who created the wounded in modern war? Madmen in suits everyone. Did the Magi really come bearing gifts? Gold, frankincense, and myrrh. On good days I would remain prayerful because I thought that was what the universe was communicating me to me and my mother was the catalyst. If only I could reach her prideful wuthering heights. Her beauty, her pale skin, her aquiline features, her beautiful tennis legs, her roots, and her burning intelligence. She is contagion. She is carrion. She is cruel to be kind. 'Thin. Thin. Thin. Why can't you be thin like your sister?' and then she screams with laughter. I go to my room and listen to Fiona Apple. I bang my door really loud so they all get the message. Films taught me to escape, to remain pure, prayerful, not wanting for what you need because

114

God was preparing you for what He deemed you could handle. There was some good in going to Sunday school and watching Robocop on a Saturday afternoon after paying your thirteen cents in the collection plate. Way back when you could still get videos. I wanted the happy ending, come hell or high water. Good people deserve happy endings.

At first, a woman in the bed (in the bedroom) slept there speaking nothing on disability, on alcoholism, and her wounds. I imagine now that woman could have been my mother. It probably was my mother and all I saw growing up in that hell house mad house loud house was her loss and her reaction to that. Her ongoing loss in life and all that she had was a negative reaction to that source. I don't know if my father could love her enough so that she could forget the childhood that came with her from Johannesburg alongside Winnie, Mandela, and the Rivonia Treason Trial. Alongside the suffering that came knocking on that door like a manic suffragette. There is always a man waiting to be found there somewhere there in the middle of a space (any place for that matter) or a sucker for every minute. Storage, fertility, sea of hands, to have none of that waiting for you in an apocalyptic future (it is good to know I did not have any of this knowledge at nine years of age), I was so bright, shiny and new. I loved my life. Every minute of it. I was surrounded by friends. I could eat anything. I could eat cake three times a day if I wanted to. I ate bacon with the rind, chicken skins. I would tear the chicken skins off the drumsticks and sticky barbecue wings smoky and tear at them with my teeth, chewing away at them happily. My mother never had the time of day for me. She was too busy with her own life, raising my brother and sister. Handing me over to my father because she couldn't cope with me anymore. She had fallen in love with my brother like every woman does across the world when she gives birth to a boy. A younger version, a newer version of her father or husband. She washed her hands off me. Anorexia Nervosa, alcoholism only happened in the movies way back then. They made addiction look so pretty. I only watched films on television. My laughter was real. It was made of substance. Something so authentic. I would sit on my father's lap and watch the news without any understanding of it. I believed in love as I believed in Oscar Micheaux, Stanley Kubrick and Orson Welles and stream of consciousness writing, and the blended family. As I grew up, surveyed the rites, the passage that was open not to every woman, not to every girl. You see unlike everyone else, the other women in my father's family I loved to read, to educate myself. I even read textbooks which were just things to other people. My father was that most rare thing in my life. He was gold. He gave me everything. He was a principal at a high school in a sub-economic area. Why is it always the vulnerable or loss that speaks to us? I waited forever for someone to sprinkle moon dust in my hair like in The Carpenter's song. But no birds suddenly appeared when the object of any of my adolescent affections were near. Oh, what a tragedy that played out to be over and over and over again. When I began to starve myself it began to affect, impact areas of my life that only in retrospect (decades later) I became aware of. It spoiled the child in me, that sweet, lovely inner child. It roughly stained my innocence through and through with a distorted view of my body image, my self-esteem and how other people saw me, the modern world's opinion of me. I am not making this up (the deep pain I felt, having the sensibility of it, of starving my body of important nutrients, pouring over the ingredient list on the back of the creamy mayonnaise bottle or of any salad dressing, drowning wilting lettuce leaves in it in order to stay alive and perky, in order to stay just peachy) to destroy any positive-minded thinking you might have on people who are disabled. Disability is not pretty. There's nothing gorgeous about it. Survival is gorgeous. The line where brutality meets goodness. The line found in solitude. The source of solitude.

Your girl is beautiful man always in motion, tethered to the generous union of the stars. Years have passed. Their novelty has still now not yet worn completely off. And there's been an awakening of sorts inside of me, inside of that festering internal me for so long. A kind of effortless pointless struggle (that seems pointless in the beginning, pointless juggling or acrobatics) but turns out to be a Darwinian revolution. Girls sing Cyndi Lauper's 'just wanna have fun'. Smoke nestles gravely in the air near her face from this thinner version of me, less of everything you got that right. You're the expert who maps out the world, intimacy speeded up on her face, her physical body, her spiritual being. Everybody in the office knows you are sleeping with her.

My aunt was one of the most sophisticated and most beautiful women I had ever met but she was also an alcoholic. Addiction ran in the family. Nobody spoke about it. It was as if we had our own secret society. On Sundays we would go to church. She was a wife. She had daughters. There are always lessons in the mysteries of life. If there are ancient lives under Botswana's sky then you can find rainbows everywhere even in Sudan. We would go to the Catholic Church in Mbabane, Swaziland. If only I had travelled more in those days. Durban was a few hours' drive away as was Mozambique. There were wonderful museums and galleries, restaurants, little cafes where you could have coffee but teenagers only wanted to go out dancing those days over the weekends and watch terrible films with their friends where they could laugh at someone else's misfortune. Nothing is set in stone. Everything is set in stone when it comes to a blood relative. You mourn for them when they're making a terrible and life-altering mistake and say, 'This too shall pass'. And when you lose them, when Death comes for them, when Eternity, eternal life comes for them or hell and damnation and you're overwhelmed with grief and denial of losing them too soon, saying it was before their time then that too shall pass. Life is like that.

The Depth Awaits

Pink watermelon flush in each cheek. Why didn't you love me mum? Are you aware of the storm you created, rain pouring down, my heart feels as if red lace is wrapped around a stone, a canvas, the painter's sketchbook? There's an odd fairy lightness in her body, my sister's body. There is no connection between us. No longer any sibling rivalry. And so the image of the autumn chill is always on my mind. Leaves all set for death and their diverse origins - destination for a cool wilderness landscape that feels like a frozen North American lake. I remember the despair and hope in the eyes of young girls thinking they are wearing fashionable clothes. I remember the range of peace, the delicate flutter of the eyes of old women, the limbs now infirm, who long for the warm sea when they used to go swimming as young girls. I remember the love song in silence when I felt I could no longer escape him. How does he move in the lovesick world now? I am the ice woman, frozen to her core, wrecked. See the descriptions of the clowns at the circus. I am one of them now and forever.

There was a sane life, an insane life, a reality, a past regret, a mistake that was made, a telephone call, an apology, laughter, past energies in a story and I was left to wonder how some people find love in this world. A love that is as ancient as rain, the apron in the kitchen amongst pots and pans, a feast-meal on the table on Sunday, daddy sitting on his throne. Childhood is lost on me, dead to adult me, past is past yet it still has such sweetness, its dissolve. And some nights it comes back, awful, familiar, all the gruesome stories with such clarity that I know it is not my imagination's spell playing tricks on me. I want it to wash away all my sins, destination anywhere, instead it says, 'Remember me. It doesn't matter who

118

you love, who you fall for, who and what you desire or drink (alcoholic), watch the men dissolve. They won't come back.' And when the awful becomes too close for comfort I take to my bed after drawing the curtains, leaving the windows open for cool air, closing the bedroom door and I will lay on the bed until I can feel notes on grief begin to vibrate within me, as if they have a quiet, harmonic society and how beautiful and sad their symphony sounds to me. It is a breathing lesson, a lesson on suffering, on living, on life. What is brutality here? It is nothing but a memory, an interruption, and becoming a mute daughter. The flick of a belt buckle, a stinging wet cloth held under a tap of cold water, mummy, mummy's red hands, mummy's gardening hands inside the chilled earth, hard laughter, harsh words, running to daddy, feet bare. He is shouting at mummy. I look at her for the first time now and I see that she is tired. Her hands hang limply at her sides now. She says nothing. My skin feels as if it is burning all over. Daddy I am burning. Daddy I am crying. I am pink all over, then red. My skin feels raw, itchy. It feels as if I am Joyce Carol Oates's harvesting flesh. She says nothing. She simply turns around and walks away. What did I do? What did I do? Where is the key to that country? How strange is the marriage of the mind to harvesting? The mind means education, psychology, something must be taught and something must be understood. To harvest means to bring closure to a season. This is what family means. To eat in front of the television, to scream and scream and scream until you cannot scream anymore. Nobody will come to you, comfort you.

And so I grew up, moved up, moved away from the world of a child and the games of the child and the adolescent and stopped believing that she lived a secret life. Perhaps mummy had a secret lover. She was beautiful in that way, easily bored in that way, did not find the same things that daddy found relevant and beautiful. They were from two different worlds. They were from two different cultures. She came from money and he didn't. She came from Johannesburg and knew a specific way of life from there. My mother came with a Pandora's Box, suitcases packed full of clothes from there when she arrived as a newlywed. My father came from Everywhere in Port Elizabeth. South End, Walmer, Fairview, North End, Korsten, a fisherman's village called Port Elizabeth, Gubb's Location, New Brighton, Zwide, Kwazakhele, Nelson Mandela Bay. Through the years those names became lodged in my memory as I studied his research wanting very much to hold onto it rather than send it to the archives at the University of the Western Cape (my father the political activist learning how to send messages using invisible ink), read his diaries from his London and European experience (I rediscovered him, his suicidal illness, and by this time I was enchanted by his depression, watched slides of the palaces he visited but I could never imagine myself there. It was enough for me to see Versailles as a tiny photograph held up against the light. He witnessed many great things, magnificent things of wonder. Daddy was wonderful in those days, a thinker, an intellectual, a teacher, a role model to me who brought me back to poetry.

Because a fire was in my head like the studies of the Whitehead poems I had begun to write because a flash of winter was in my head. Like the chains of bitterness in a veteran photographer's memory but there was also something unfinished inside of me, something had dissolved. Look for opportunities the guardian band of gold around the sun said and that became my mission's. I began to imagine other people's shackles of pain, their chains, their prison walls put up all around them, the spirit of fear, hurt and rejection within them, abandonment, and spiritual neglect, poverty and for some reason it felt like I was multiplying gravity.

I got tired of people asking me to smile please, you'd be lovelier if you did.

Did I have courage, that mute child in the photograph? I've suffered but what is suffering anyway when compared to others. I have a mental switch but what do others have? What are their coping mechanisms? The universe gives freely to me. I have refuge if I want it. I have a sanctuary if I

120

want it. Hope is there. In the arrival of it there is always freedom. There is always revolution in the mind of the poet and quintessence in the poetry that comes from the mouth, the voice, the straightforward thinking of that kind of revolution.

I've met someone else. He tells me everything. He isn't afraid to tell me anything. And slowly the veil lifts my smile and becomes like a scar. My wounds are like stigmata. And I begin to see and hear everything again. Hope floats. There are angels everywhere yet I still feel incomplete like some kind of show off finding it tiresome to live normally like the people next door who weren't embarrassed to get drunk in front of their children. I'm embarrassed by loneliness, despair and my bleak outlook on life. I know where you've been once upon a secret life. A secret life. Do insects have secret lives too and what is their best intention for all those years they live with secrets? Therein lies their survival. When my sister comes home she and my mother sit down together as if it was the most normal thing in the world and they drink. They drink cocktails. Pink syrupy liquids that seem to sparkle, sparkling wines, Peach schnapps', vodka and orange juice cool as ice going down their throats. I prefer my secret life.

As an adult my mother, mummy is no longer my morning star and my sister is still my dream stealer. They have become my life, guarding the car keys and the bottle of milk stout. I have to find my own projects. According to God's plan he wants us, me to act accordingly, justly, with integrity, humility. He wants us to go forth into the new world knowing that He is always on our side now and forever more.

We're all born with a philosophy, not necessarily a Plan B so to speak, and we want to bring meaning to our own lives. I found a book once called Norah's Secret Life and as I was reading it I discovered many things about this woman whose life I wouldn't exactly call exciting or romantic. She had 'romantic' love affairs but they were doomed from the start. She was or

121

wasn't significant but her life seemed to become something symbolic as if I had to have an opportunistic use for it later on in life.

She was unfortunately not the marrying kind but she had a wealth of spiritual knowledge unlike any other woman of her generation and sometimes in the love affairs she had she would think like a man when it came to the 'transaction'. In the material world men dominated she knew she could never win. And so she became like the smiling faces of children amidst poverty. When she wanted to escape, she did what all men did, she educated herself, she painted, and she received visitors, she wrote unfathomable poetry that was never self-pitying but stories that were in a way. And in one way, perhaps some ways she became the caretaker of so many women who lived in isolation of a society who would not accept them because they chose to live an unconventional life.

At the end of one her love affairs Norah seems to be coping with her new life as best she can like the stars in the evening sky when the earth smells clean and as fresh and new as vanilla. She is bright. Her spirit feels bright. It feels too bright. Her conversation can be illuminating and clever. She wants to be entertained. She wants to be filled with joie de vivre. She also wants to be pursued. Doesn't any woman want to be pursued? Men are extraordinary when they are in pursuit. They have a grand perspective. They regale you with stories. The world becomes magnificent when they're in it with you on their arm and you're going places. It doesn't really matter that you're part of his secret life. They're still pretty impressive. They make you feel desired, beautiful, and the grief that you once felt or had so strongly in your life above anything else is no longer triumphant. You're no longer flying-walking-singing-chanting solo.

It is the year 2013, nearly two in the morning, December and another Christmas have come and gone and my brother is about to become a father. I can't mock him anymore. And in the exquisite compass of the infinite internal struggle between suicide, wanting to fly, wanting to have

122

that family, that plan coming together, the memory, the thought of Plath, Hughes, Bessie Head, Anne Sexton, Robert Lowell I am still here. I am alive with an awakened spirit, with everything that I've put the sum parts of me through I have realised that I cannot turn back. I have to move on, move forward because I 'm the sun's mistress and life after all is a mission. I don't really see how my life could change after this, after all I've put it through. Two birds. Plath and Sexton. Once upon a time they were two birds on a mission too. Joy fills my lungs so does a surge for the realisation of humanity. Our survival. Our instinct. The little one's name is Reuben. We're all actors acting in a bit part there and a bit part here. My brother held this bright shining thing in his arms. Something that would be educated, instilled with his values, his parenting skills and I felt as if I was being torn apart by some primal, primitive animalistic force. And I knew that I would put the past Jean Rhys's, Mr Mackenzie's (plural) behind me. I never had an ounce of ambition within me anyway. They had all come with the world's territory. There it was. The undocumented love affair was really most of all inside my head however brilliant the man was and however bold his moves and brave I was to take him on.

I knew something different now. I was more defiant like Norah was in her secret life because eventually she had found her way out. Nobody wants the ending of a book or film to be spoiled for them. Norah had found her way out and she was happy. As happy as could be. Women deserve to be happy. Men are altogether different. Lost boys everyone. They are always searching. I don't think they ever grow up.

Female nude

They ate fried chicken on Monday but on Friday he liked a steak with his hot tea and chips. This was before I came along screaming blue in the face. On their walk on a Saturday afternoon through the park they would stop for a light picnic lunch (usually a variety of sandwiches and ice tea or cold lemonade, let me stop here. On Sundays she would curl up on the sofa and read her cookbooks after the greasy feast of roast chicken and he would sit in his study and read the newspapers. Tall men have such a sweetness about them even boys. Tall men have such a sweetness about them. My father was not a tall man. My mother's love, mummy (that's what I called her) was like a cold photocopy. Why do women long for children anyhow? Is it biology or survival or do they mean the same thing? I'm just a woman who longs for a child of her own now but the pretty are way more advanced than I am. They've married happily or unhappily and they've had those kids.

The red seed of an abortion flowing out of the woman's body. Nobody talks about backstreet abortions anymore in Johannesburg. You can go to any clinic. The red seed growing and growing cancer cells. How can I be delivered from those things? How can I escape, forget? I ran away before to another city but I don't think I can do that again. I'm too grown up. I am too set in my ways.

I'm safe here. Amongst these houses. In this house. In this suburb. The elite. Those are two words that mean absolutely nothing to me. What does being wealthy mean for humanity at large? It is a meagre one percent. I do not count myself amongst them. It is not my money. It doesn't belong to me. I didn't work for it. I've wasted years, energy on a variety of things. I tried to educate myself but the real world is a machine and it spits you out if you do not fit. If you're unconventional. If you're ugly and emotional. Sylvia Plath is so beautiful, all her doll parts. I'm obsessed with her. I eat to live. I eat to live, to survive another day in modern society although it stinks to high heaven with shadows and insecurity.

The house belongs to my parents. My brother is fixing it up. His son's name is Ethan. His girlfriend's name is Rose. He does some painting. He has a patch of garden where he is growing vegetables. He says we are going all out organic in a big way. We have to eat healthily. He is so handsome but now he is taken. All the girls wanted him. They danced around him. All he had to do was to click his fingers. He could have anyone. I had all these dreams of living in a world-drama like that.

I am rich in other ways. I see now that spiritually I am richer. I mean to say that perhaps in the beginning stages of my life, in the formative years my mental faculty was not as rich as it is now.

Johannesburg smells. It smells of poo, dirt, urine, pavement meeting rain, thunderstorms, white snow spreading out like a blanket, smoke, people, blood, cars, trains, pollution, mines, funerals, murders, and films. I love films. Faster, faster, faster is how everything goes there.

I know you. I've always known you. You knew that then and you know that now. I am not coming for you anymore. You're history, remember. Funny how we never said that word goodbye as if we were both reaching for something. Are you lost heathen?

I want to write to her, my sister who wants to travel the world but I do not want to write to her, not of suffering, loss, sadness, the mourning period, a stolen kiss in the cemetery and not the peck on the cheek kind. I want to be overwhelmed by the brethren's kindness. I know she won't reply though. She's the pretty one. She's the one I make most nervous.

How I work on her acute dopamine and serotonin levels. Shame on me. Shame on her.

During the cocktail hour in my house the world becomes a new place. Mummy and Sissy. And then there's a calm breeze that floats through the house. Sissy is short for sister. The awfully good middle child. The achiever. Invincible Superwoman. I have a rush of love for her. For mummy too even when she's at her terrifying worst. The vodka loosens the tongue. I can hear laughter, cackling even. They've finished the orange juice and that makes me mad. They know I can't drink the strong stuff, the heavy stuff. What do to with madness except admit defeat and sink?

I don't think I've ever felt brave enough to feel that vulnerable in front of someone else. Man, woman, child did it matter.

You who do not know me, of me, what I have carried for years, the internal struggle I have been in, had to spirit away while nations have been at war I think of your kindness. You came like a thief in the night.

Focus on what I am trying to tell you. The January heat of the sun is pinned to my cheek, there are tears building up inside of me like sap when I remember you. Golden-gorgeous-genius you as much of a lover of words as I am. And when I think of magnificent you, that incredible phase in my life (past is past but still you are not dead to me and still further along you are not a ghost) I think of you as a cure, an anchor, a door that is left ajar for a visitor, and when I think of you I drown but not in despair or shame (blush of red on my cheeks).

I drown in hope. I forget that you killed me once, perhaps on more than one occasion. Write. Write words. Anything that takes your fancy, pleases you, makes you glad and see the loveliness in the world. Now that's a mantra. Smile. Pick up the fragments, the small bits and little pieces. Sylvia Plath wrote about kindness and words, their purity, clarity, poetry, dryness. It came like a flood out of her, pouring out like machinations,

126

sunshine, liquid, the blue jewel of the sky. I think it became necessary for her in a way like writing has become necessary for me. I need you Sissy but you're not there. You're not connected to me in the substantial way we were once as children. Sometimes I call her Jean in my stories or Eve. I'm scared. I do not want to go back there again, held hostage by deep pain and regret. Where are these words coming from? I do not know. To question it means the death of me. You don't know anything about me. I prefer it that way because if you knew anything about me it would mean the death of you. I'm awfully mean. I'm a miserable person. I'm miserable company to be around with. I am not an idol or a celebrity. I am not a god or a leader of a secret cult. So do not worship me. Food for thought. I will let you down. I cannot nurture anything. I will let you down badly. Keep your expectations to yourself. You in all your loveliness, splendour and wonder I surmise will need it more than I do.

I've never been good enough for this world. It has pushed me aside to get to the pretty ones. The lovely ones. Popular, not so moral ones but they have not stood the tests of time. They do not pray. They aren't churchgoers. They aren't Christian or even Catholic or even Muslim girls. They who delve into having their dope smoking 'man-of-the-year'. They are the visible ones. How can they be lonely when they have nothing in their heads but moth smoke, and heat and it has lived there so long that cobwebs have sprung up, a kind of witch's brew to drown their spirits when they are feeling pointless. When their perspective is lost. Oh, lots of people say they aren't good enough for this world but they're simply lying to themselves. Sometimes even the beautiful get lost. So lost in fact that they land in the wards of hell. I don't pity them for a minute. They found their own way there and must make their own way back to the universe that created them. I am talking about those people who are lost-lost. Just plain lost. They came into the world this way. Deserted by family. Perhaps there was an absent mother, an absent father, or perhaps they witnessed violence (I've witnessed violence and made stories up about it.) They are

127

Immortals every single one of them. They suck 'blood' (conversation, acting in a world-drama) from mortals, suck water from rivers (the sea is filled salt and salt robs them of feeling physical, their angelic otherworldliness) because they're thirsty (as if it is the first time they have felt it on their skin), and feed on chicken feet. They cherish red meat. They're a butcher's wife every one of them. How I hated them? Their soft mouths, the apple in their cheeks, the paradise I believed that men and boys would receive when they spoiled these 'children' to get to love, to say those words and mean it and to say those words and not mean it anymore.

The lost girls do not know how to remember loss, suffering, suicidal illness, confessional poetry, what comes after silence, the passing of history, death, poverty. They do not know what the meaning of the words genocide or Holocaust is.

They know that autumn comes before winter. They have devoted themselves to making themselves look like the cover of a magazine. It's a tragedy. Comedy speeded up. You can still get a sadistic pleasure out of it, watching them. Studying them up close and personal. Observing their habits 'in the wild' (their most natural environment which is the bathroom).

If only they had the brains. If only I had the patience to teach them. If only they could understand. If only they could surprise me these half-wits, these idiots with their shiny pink lips that they continually go to the bathroom and dot more lipstick on because they are expecting a man to show up. It is so hot here. I am sinking. I am becoming more and more lost. And I can't help it.

Parents have their favourites. I am my father's favourite. It didn't matter to the world, to the charismatic older men I met in that dumb world fuelled by money and ambition, the feel of their skin, to the boys (schoolboys tripping on acne, and hormones), to the other girls, the girls who were the same as me, to women, to women who were as cold, as frozen as my mother. She never had a warm embrace for me. She never had a kind word to say to me. And if she did it was for her own pleasure. As if all she did was make me and that was enough, handing me over to my father to raise. I wasn't really a woman or a girl at the end of youth. This, this was normal and when I found out it wasn't. When I was fifteen or fourteen it killed something inside of me. It shattered me. It destroyed me. And I became as I wrote in Bittersweet Squalor a destroyer. I became the queen of bitter and mean. I became nasty and nothing that I did could flip that switch. Up and down. Up, up, up and then down, down as if I was a drug addict on uppers and downers.

I have learned the hard way that it's important to most of all to have a passion to write and then that burst of black clouds, that approaching storm, that half-buried voice inside of me that demands to be crazy and heard at the same time (lunatic make peace with the world I say) doesn't exist anymore. It doesn't have a soul. It doesn't have a spirit. It doesn't have a physical, mental or emotional body. You can't act your way out of an acute spell of depression. So the love affair ended. The older man moved on to the birthday of his son and his life, his eloquent wife. How articulate he was in saying and not saying all of these things to me. A killer is a killer is still a killer. Was I too much masculine, not feminine enough?

All of these questions will drive me insane or to an early grave.

Are you trying to make a statement by doing that, going out like that?

Would you prefer me to be lonely, stay in on Friday and Saturday nights with oh-so-serious-you?

Wipe that smirk off your face. You're sly. You're very, very sly? You're a fox. You're a red fox. And you're going on a hunt. Are you going on a hunt femme fatale?

I'm what?

You're something else. Come here. I want to remind you that you're a married woman. You do not have options. I am your husband and you have to obey me.

Oh. Now I see the choices that I have.

And? Dance. I want you to dance. Spin around. Put some fresh lipstick on and then kiss me.

No. You're talking crazy. Why don't you get up from that sofa lazybones and make me? Why not dance with me?

Why don't you join me on the sofa?

I'm not in the mood. I'm starting to hate you. I'm a lover not a hater. Oh, he gets a smile for that one. I wonder what my reward will be.

I'm starving. I'm going to make a sandwich. Put on some music for us and I'll get a bottle of red.

Are you thinking what I'm thinking?

No, no and no.

I just want cake.

You have to start watching what you're eating some time so why not now?

A tiny piece of gorgeous cake made by my gorgeous wife then I'll keep the peace.

You promise?

Don't I always keep my promises?

Depends.

Depends on what?

I guess the planets mostly. The price of a loaf of bread. America. Conspiracy theorists.

Come here.

No.

Look at me.

No.

Come here. Just turn your head. You can still see me.

Why can't you just say what you want to say to me? I can hear you from where I'm standing.

Real people do not talk like that. Do newlyweds talk like that? Do people who have stayed married for thirteen years talk like that? I know that in Terms of Endearment they did not talk like that. Nor in August: Osage County. Someone died in each of those movies. Someone loved. Someone special and funny. Someone who had a unique spirit. I know that real people don't talk like that but sometimes I imagine that they do when I feel as if I have a peculiar spirit or nature. Lie. Lie. Lie. Liar. What I meant to say was when I feel sad, gripped by it, carried to its threshold, when it speaks to me, when my head is wrapped tightly around it, can't get loosened from it. In my head I would make up the conversations we would have over a period of nearly thirteen years of married life. Are vows terms, conditions? Will we go to church or lie in on Sunday mornings with our cold toast complete with gloop of shining marmalade with its pretty sun face, lukewarm milky tea and the newspapers reading our favourites. You will tuck a stray brown curl of hair behind the lobe of my ear, kiss it. Say, 'You're really sweet. You smell lovely. All perfumery.' Later on, you will go and make us coffee (my pretend husband will go and make me coffee and yes only in my dreams) before we go out for a walk on the beach. We will hold hands. You will put your arm around my waist. We will look into each other's eyes, talk about our week at work, about our friends at work. Someone will say something funny. We will both guffaw like crazy. We don't have children. We have accepted that we can't have any. It isn't anybody's fault really (this really means it's my fault. It's impossible for me, for my genes). We have a dog called Misty Upham after this beautiful Native American girl who played the role of a beautiful Native American nurse and cook in the film August: Osage County. You (my husband) have a dog. I have a cat. Kitty. Cat for short. In real life my cat is dead. Tender is the day, the salt on the breeze catching my hair, the nape of my neck, and the backs of our legs. You're laughing and complaining at the same time, that I decided we come out today of all days. We've both rolled up our pants. We're eating vanilla ice cream with a chocolate flake inside of it. You've picked me up. I'm screaming. Screaming with joy and terror. It's cold. The sea has always freaked me out. I can swim. I just prefer to swim in a heated pool, preferably indoors. I hate the smell of chlorine, the sight of skinny people, so wrapped up in the joy of their thinness and revealing it to the world at large. There's something beloved about my local swimming pool. I've been swimming there since I've been a child with my mother and father, my two younger siblings.

Beetroot. Coleslaw. Fried chicken. All of this in front of you a feast. A huge serving. Not like those portions you're used to getting at the clinic. The portion that could fit into your hand. Now eat. Eat as much as you like or eat as little but you have to eat some. Put it on the end of your fork and now eat this stuff. Some of it is healthy and some of it is unhealthy. Just for you, I added extra Tabasco and mayonnaise. Beetroot, coleslaw, chicken is the colour of the day. It will brighten you up. You look so pale because you haven't been eating right. The doctors spoke about this. Your therapist. You can't push people who care about you, who are concerned about you and your episodes of mild clinical depression away from you. Just think that not so long ago this was your favourite meal at the hospital. You couldn't eat anything at that posh clinic. Just think what will happen if you don't eat. You'll simply fade away, waste away to absolutely nothing but skin and bone like those kids in Ethiopia, Somalia, wherever-in-Africa. Ethiopia's in Africa right? See I made you smile. History was never my strongest subject in school or is that Geography. See how I made you laugh. Look at me. A regular stand-up comedian. You're a moron if you don't eat this. I'm going to have to throw this good stuff away. I can't eat all of it. It'll go off in the fridge. Are you listening to me or am I losing you?

Hey, don't tell me I can't click my fingers in your face. I need you to pay attention to me. Listen you. You have to start eating and putting on some weight. This kind of lifestyle is not doing anything for you. This negativity. It's just being selfish. You're being selfish. Can't you see that? I hate this. I hate wearing this hat. It is making me tired. You playing these games. These mind games. You can play them with your doctors, the other patients, your psychologist, the occupational therapist then that is fine by me but you can't come home like this. You can't come home to me like this. I am your husband. You're not behaving. If you don't know how to behave like a wife, a proper wife, then what will happen to both of us? You're sabotaging us. Something close to perfection. Marriage is not perfect but it can be happy. It can make both people realise that they aren't perfect people. You're making us, the once upon a time perfect us unhappy. Don't do this. Just do the small things. It's not such a big deal to have a meal. It's not as if I'm asking you to eat three times a day. This is just the beginning of a very long road to sanity. Forget about being sophisticated. Forget about vanity. Maybe I'll give up on you today but I won't give up on you tomorrow and that's just the way it is. I was saving the vanilla ice cream for you. You'll find it in the freezer.

133

And then he ends the conversation like that. He switches off the lights in the kitchen brooding and brooding and brooding. And then the brooding turns to bitterness and then rots and festers in his heart or wherever bitterness, rotting and festering takes place. My dreamy pretend husband leaves me in the darkness of our perfect kitchen that I picked out of the pages of a magazine. Imagination is a wonderful thing. The thing is I am not even looking for a husband. And that is the wicked truth of it all.

In the thirtieth year a nephew has come along, a girlfriend has moved all her flat's furniture into our house, my parents' house and I begin to hate, rot and fester more and more. This is me speaking and not my imagination. Life begins to become more brutal, less forgiving. God, how it wounds. This aggression. Life aggravates me and my nerves. It feels like lightning and electricity combined. Can you even imagine that kind of catalyst communicating to the world of the dead? All the suffering. All the details. All I want is God to speak to me. On the other hand, words speak to me also. I grasp at them like my nephew's hands grasp at nothing and everything. And when that voice comes it comes in moth-speak, fog evaporating, leaves tearing up districts, Whitman's blades of grass, rain meeting pavement, making it wet, slick, making hair wet, slick, licking umbrellas, shoes, coats. It comes with the wind that shakes up everything in its path. I remember how the Johannesburg people wanted to take my father away from me, from Port Elizabeth, my brother, my mother and me. Mostly me I think. They thought we wanted his money. How cruel. People are cruel (here I mean family). Love ones to loved ones. The closest to you. I don't believe in worshipping family anymore. Scratch that one law, rule, resolution out. It doesn't mean anything to me anymore. Relationships and everything else were blackened that September and October. 2013. 2013 taught me that pretend was just play-play, another child's jubilant playing field. And now we come to nearly thirteen years of leaping and awe-inspiring loneliness etched into every landscape that I've travelled through, every wonder I've quietly observed, every childhood that has burned to the ground, every passion that felt like a fever, that has taken on the guise of a pretty flower in a garden that has made your spirit felt charged and ready for success, every three-leafed clover sorely missing its fourth. Now we come to thirteen years of depressive suicidal illness and disability. Thirteen years of emotional instability. Ups and downs. Follow the writer. The twit. The twitter. The twittering. Follow the babble, the kerfuffle. Follow the leader. Play reader. Play. Push the red button. Drift. That is what it comes down to. Just drift because that is what humanity is meant to do when facing off the physical. When the physical becomes nasty, mean-spirited. And all it gives your brain is negative information, wishes that will never come true no matter how hard you wish for it, no matter how long you hold your breath. It feeds your brain ugly myths and unfortunately there is nothing of the fairy-tale kind where good always triumphs over evil, where I am good, good enough.

I loved you. I always will. For thirteen years now I've loved you, met up with you again, again and again in my dreams for real and not pretend and sometimes it kills me to say it. You're somebody else's husband. Somebody else's fella. Some days are good. Some days are bad. God has married the romantic gentleman you to my memories like the world around me has grown to become more digital. It just goes faster. I have no control over it. There's no function key that I can press. My contemporaries are far more advanced than me. I've come to terms with that. I still don't know anything about you. I don't know who you are. What you think about when you lie awake at night in your bedroom next to your lovely wife who is nothing, nothing like me. Is she ordinary-extraordinary? Lie. Lie. Lie. Liar. You were my best friend. My only friend as it turned out to be. You taught me truth was the only policy to live by. Some kind of special gentleman you were. You offered me some kind of hope, self-esteem, and culture in a zoo of players. For some time now you have made me very happy. I've starved myself for so long. Can you understand what I am trying to tell you? I am never coming back, going back.

135

You made me quite ill. Frighteningly so. I scared myself to death. I was high on you. Addicted to your kind of human nature, funny hint of environment, scarcity of empathy (did you even know what the word sympathy meant or did it just mean having a sexual transaction to you).

Jean Rhys

I can hear his voice in my veins. He calls me his, 'Porcelain-darling'.

Sometimes in my flat here in London I would move from one room to the next astonished at this 'love-experiment' I was delving into. I was now once again 'a work in progress' as I had been as a child in Dominica. The first man I ever loved made me feel more of an exile on these London streets. Far away from home, the only home I had ever known. It was the known. Love is like plasma, floating mitochondria, atomic particles, the accurate building up of ignorance into life experience, the harsh, neon underground bricks of illness.

Love for me was always an unlikely dilemma. Do I or don't I? Sometimes I think we live with ghosts. Love is a ghost. It is ancient as illness but it makes me bleed at the starting line. Curtains at the open window of the hotel room are moving in sync with my little bleeding scarlet heart. Why do I write? I want to find myself in eternity when I'm in heaven. Everything has returned to normal. I am on my own again. I don't want to strike it rich or land me a guy to marry me (both at the same time would be a dream).

There will be no reunions with family, with lovers, with 'him', that kind, sincere wealthy man I first met when I was such an ingénue. He taught me the difference between the words, 'authentic', 'squalor', 'but these are terrible living conditions', and 'you can even find human nature in a symphony if you listen close enough'. He taught me the meaning of words like, 'the brittle movements and accurate moments of solitude', 'how to be astonished at how ignorant people were, how vain women and men were', 'all pictures always carried powerful observations of life in the details'.

I would hear his voice everywhere I went in the beginning stages of our relationship (I called our little affair). His voice healed some parts of me especially when the dark air of night was advancing.

'God is mostly in your head but most people do what their hearts tell them to do.' 'Life is boring and we need activities like love to get us through the day. We're a match. People think life owes them something if they're not born rich but even rich people are lonely and ignorant. They can go to the best schools in the world, but are they educated, no, cultured, no. Have you ever felt abandoned, neglected, ill at the thought of being rejected (I felt like that my whole childhood) I wanted to ask but was too afraid to, too afraid he would think I was a mouse, weak? There was clarity in that.

You need to think more of yourself, Jean love. You need to express yourself. If you feel indignant, feel indignant. If you feel confident, feel confident. Don't be so afraid of the world around. What is the worst thing that could happen (I already knew, that someone could laugh in my face, stare me down until I looked away but I never confided this in him because there was no reason to)? Sometimes I think you feel terribly lost. I see a terror in your eyes as we leave one another. You remind me of a lotus flower and for me it is the most beautiful flower in the world.

He could I articulate it (love), show it, examples of it (I could only describe it, make plans for it for the most part in my head, connecting threads of the purest thoughts of it in black notebooks). I was his pretty doll whom he spoke of in whispers to in the dark.

Jean, sometimes I think you are hiding something away from me. I think an entire wonderland must exist inside your head for your own pleasure. What sweetness that must come with. It must taste refreshing. It

138

must taste like pink happiness, a deposit of charm in a room that has not felt it for days, for my Jean, my bird without wings.

And so his champagne voice would carry me through the day and for most of the night for this insomniac. Sometimes I could feel the stress on my heart, its thudding, hammering away pressure and there was nothing in the world I could do about it. All I had to do was to live. I would watch children sometimes and think to myself what their gifts to the world would be when they grew up. Sometimes my heart would turn to paste as I watched them and I would think that now, finally everything had been taken away from me. I could never be free and then I would walk down back streets.

There would always be an undeniable lightness in the road's blackness as evening began to settle all around me. Its magic fingers in my hair, the wind rearranging my hat, massaging thoughts of rope and poison, putting stones into the pockets of my coat and walking into a lake filled with ice and trees at the bottom into my mind's eye.

I would think of the dilemma that faced Romeo and Juliet and how sometimes when I was feeling very low how that same dilemma faced me. I wanted to be myself but not on my own like this. I knew I had failed. I did not know how to get back to life.

I did not know how to dance to modern society's beat. I did not know what modern meant anyway but I knew I was a most modern woman attached to absolutely nobody and nothing. And then the tears would come streaming down my face. I could not stop them and why I. Life would have not been fair to me. I did not know anything about modern acrobatics and the flying trapeze artist was a comic to me and sometimes my mind's eye was a width of a thread and it was simply connected to nothing. Some days I would feel brave as if I had a destination in my step but I knew that was a lie.

Soon everywhere I went I would hear his voice in my head as if he was with me in the room. 'You can survive anything, Jean, as long as you put your heart and mind to it. You look beautiful tonight, simply divine, and come here let me hold you. It feels as if it's been forever since I've last seen you.' By that time he was already a ghost. It didn't feel real to me. His voice had no substance but it kept me company, the illusion was so strong. I didn't know how to distance myself away from that habitat of his beautiful house filled with fireplaces, flowers and pictures hanging on the walls of landscapes, a wine cellar. I just wanted to dissolve.

Sometimes you live poverty. I've lived in poverty. And at first, I didn't want people to see me like that. You know, drab, pathetic, old clothes, out of fashion. Funny, but it made a difference to them, made their hearts and their diplomatic hearts and heads softer towards me. They exhibited empathy for what I always thought was my unlikely demise. They gave me money and I would use it to live as best I could. There was an understanding. Out of sight, out of mind. It was fine if I was going out of my mind with loneliness so long as it was on their terms.

And when a guy (I really don't really know his name, how we met), finally he broke off the affair a few months later he was very diplomatic and suave about it. Although I couldn't understand how he could be so composed about the whole deal. To them money meant success. I had no money. I wished sometimes that I could distance myself away from it, my love for it but I needed to live as other people did, don't you see. Whatever that word 'normal' meant it gave me Goosebumps just thinking about it. And then, in the end, I thought it was normal to distance myself from society.

From London to Paris, Europe what a pilgrimage, what a privilege. Whoever gets the chance to travel these days? And then I was soon back in London again. Whatever happened in Paris had been an adventure but now it was over. Sometimes I felt vertigo as I was walking on those London streets. I felt blessed with the knowledge that somehow I was perhaps writing for a generation that would come years after me in a golden age. It was a generation who was now experiencing life as children while I was a grown woman. Sometimes I thought to myself I was not meant for this world.

In the evenings London would become a ghost nation but I did not want to be stuck in a room. It was too depressing. I became too aware of my current situation. It would make me feel sad. I would feel like having a drink and then my whole outlook on life would change after I had the drink within me. The man who lived below me would knock a broom into his ceiling and ask me to 'keep it down in there' (whatever the hell that meant). I didn't know what on earth I got up to in the early hours of the morning. Sometimes I thought I would just be writing, scribbling away, staring at the walls. I would think about love, how much I really liked the idea of it.

There are a lot of things in this world that are rotten, unpleasant things to deal with. In the evening or usually when I am alone something always seems to lose itself violently from me. Sadness, a wounded feeling as if I almost don't belong in this world and in a way I know I don't fit. Perhaps I am too reckless in the choices that I make. Perhaps I am not a safe person to be around. Too much of a thinker, brooder, reader always keeping love and the attraction of it in the dark until I can feel pinpoints of lights trying to break through the cracks. I am no good. I am bad at love.

I am bad at affairs and matters of the heart and bad at relationships. I must rest now. Tomorrow is another day. So I wait until the room is filled with darkness and I listen to the noises in the street outside, downstairs, in my own room. And I know I've walked that street today like a ghost as if I was not aware of my surroundings. Soup is always good for the soul, as are confessions. Here is one for one. I don't believe in the death of things anymore. I believe in life as much as that is hard to believe. If only someone knew me well. If only I had a companion.

If only I didn't have to suffer for my art. All of my life I watched women in their relationships with men. How they would smile, turn their head, their eyes watchful and waiting, how they would smooth their hair down, arrange the food, the salad on the plate or cast their eyes over a menu and how the men were pensive, eager to please in this sunny environment. How could I have known then as a child that I was not one of them? And that I was never going to grow up and be one of them? I would watch these women always smiling; listening (but were they really listening).

And I wondered why these women with their fine clothes, elaborate hats, and brooches why never spoke back. They were always nodding their heads like puppets. I knew from an early age I was not too pretty so I would have to work hard, but also I would have to discipline myself not to be too smart. I reckoned that people's lives are meant to be celebrated when they're alive not dead. There was always something pure about the day as I set about my walk and there is something to be celebrated in that. The union of life mixed with the elixir of what I drank (and I always thought of it as an elixir).

I was not built like that, to be tough I mean. I was never meant to be a bully or a tyrant. I just did not have that warmth in my voice, that kind of spirit flowing in my blood. If poetry is an elixir then prose is food for thought. I've walked past people and they've stared at me. I've looked away but sometimes when I really think of getting to grips with the situation I want them to try and understand me so I stare back. What do they see, a casualty disconnected from the rest of the world? I live so simply. My life is easy and cheap. My supper is usually bread and cheese.

It is always bread and cheese. No change there and my hands smell like soap and this room's bare-bones creak under my stockinged feet at night. Writing has become my ritual. It has become my escape from grief and raw anguish and frustration.

Sometimes the process of writing torments me but I also feel very anchored by it. It's therapeutic, it minimises the stress that I feel thudding inside my head and it gives me a sense of purpose. All the words seduce me, gets under my skin. It is so intense, this pleasure that unravels and seems to release the chill out of me on cold nights.

But I can no longer feel the weight of the world resting on my shoulders so acutely. The words seem to paint that blue pearl into a rainbow of magic colour. Into childlike stuff of fairies, dust, a water wonderland, into soul and life, everything of beauty and not a disturbing sense of things. I always wished as a child to make contact with things like that, magical things. I'm thirsty so I get up for some water. I can still taste the salt in the air coming in from the sea in Dominica. Why would I go back? Sometimes I remember why and sometimes I don't.

Fast forward to a flat in London and I go by the name now of Jean Rhys. A name I have changed so many times. I have no money, no skills, and no form of employment. The cheques come regularly. He called me a 'porcelain darling', 'daring good girl', 'special' and that I was 'loveliness personified'. He had kind eyes. He was so authentic and a real gentleman. I mean authentic in the terms of he was a man who was made of substance and everything around him, his home, his household, his wealth felt real to me as I entered the foyer and stared at the flowers in the vase that seemed to welcome even me.

I believed nothing was wrong and even when the affair ended, I still thought perhaps there would be contact again and even a friendship but years have passed (the poet in me I guess came up with these foolish notions). Realising that the past is passed even the temporary frightened me to death. But there had to have been some reward, something golden that I could get out of the equation of knowing this man and coming into his world even for a short period of time. I could not solely have duped myself into thinking, into believing that it was just a lack on his part.

You know that whole easy situation. I could think about these things for hours on end, fill my entire day on the "he said she said" transmission of our conversations. Sometimes I would get stuck on a sentence, just the tone, how he would express himself and it would drive me crazy, up the wall and I would will my brain to dissolve it. It would feel brutal but brutality in the end also serves its own purpose. It will make you realise that you need to rest. I don't know quite when I've finished with something. When I have to quit it but I do know when I have to rest. When I'm kaput.

It is not going to work out Jean.

You know how these things are between a man and woman.

You're not too blame.

It's just what happens in the world, it is called human nature.

One day you'll be a grown woman, a lady and you will understand all of this.

It's not easy for me to say this.

You're still young and believe me; you will fall in love again.

I'm too young to know about those sorts of things, that's what I wanted to say at the time. I was thinking it all the time watching the creases in the corners of his mouth. How the fleshy part of the skin in the middle of his forehead was crinkling up as he watched my reaction. I know he was

144

just testing me to see if I would fly out of control, would she make a scene? How would the past few months come to an end?

I felt like an orphan. I shouldn't say things like that but that is what I felt like. Lost, terribly afraid of the world, neglected, abandoned, no home, no name and family.

There was no hope in damned hell to resurrect my lone self. There were parts of me that werewolfish, that was the part of me that could fight, battle (I have the scars to prove it) if I had to. No, if I was challenged. But I also withdrew easily and that was the weakest part of me. It didn't matter what kind of climate I found myself sheltered by. I embraced skating on illness and when I did I yearned the most for my art and all my little rituals. Now I am tired of the years of cold I have lived through and this incessant hunger that I feel for attention and most of all my neediness.

Violets were my favourite flowers in the world. Maybe because they're so pretty and cheerful they make me feel that way. They don't make me feel like death, volcano dust or blue warmed up. Sometimes I dream of my mother's fingers knitting, not braiding my hair. In the middle of the night I come upon a sleeping world, a dream world. I journey there for a while pacing back and forth, sometimes crying, sometimes in a sombre mood before I fall asleep myself. The stars are like birds in my eyes on the nights you can see stars in London.

They are like birds with their wings outstretched. Ready to meet the oncoming edge of the sky or a sword of air. All 'Ella' had was imagination and she kept that close to her. 'Ella' was always secretive and I have kept that because if I didn't I would have come undone a long time ago. I am what I am because I have wanted people to believe it, especially other women. In life there are always choices, pleasure, desires. I always kept waiting for love to change everything. A Prince charming and as dark as an Arabian knight in shining armour to rescue me.

But life never goes according to plan although I am an open door. Sometimes it feels as if I come alive in the dark. The sun is like a mirror. If it's there I never see it. I am not conscious of its light, and my reflection in it. I can feel (I've always been aware of this for what feels like forever) the dark side of life more intensely than the lighter side of the life of it.

My hair was not spun gold. It was dark. I did not believe in fairies and their wings or that Dominica was an island but I did like the trees. They were my favourite and the open fields and when a spell of tiredness came upon me, when I couldn't breathe because of the heat I would imagine. My goal became to fall in love with warriors in suits who had wonder guts in their blood. I've loved many and I've lost some along the way. Splendid confidantes that I held in high esteem as if royalty. I've learned to go on loving although it is the hard way.

You go on paying the price one too many times. There's a flaw in passion, a conspiracy in love, that hate that always cornered me on the playing fields of childhood that seemed to flow my way as a gauche chorus girl. You know once upon a time there was a man who wanted to adopt me. I think he wanted to take care of me and be a fatherly figure. Some kind of mentor, a friendly man who would keep me out of the firing line of the inquiring gazes of others who would exchange company for money. One last time I am more in love with being in love than anything else.

The air is crisp (a tattoo on the green landscape). It feels as if I am living in an ancient world collapsing under meteors. What does progress mean to a writer? Write more books but they have to have a market and they have to sell well but the writer must always be morose and depressed. Very difficult when it comes to giving interviews.

I do not know what impact my books have on the rest of the world and I would like it to stay that way. I know that human behaviour is predictable. It is also a precious cargo. But I am made of glass.

Why call off the splendid search (such an adventure) for the adventurous spirit at heart, that instinct. I am the feminine lark, the songbird. In my line of work there is such a thing as clarity but no such things as clocks. What is the meaning of that four-letter word l-o-v-e? And when it is nailed to my heart why do I stammer when I speak, why does my heart beat to another rhythm, cadence (I can hear it as if it has gone underground somewhere). I have to mine it like a mineral deposit. In love when I have fallen, fallen hard all my thoughts are hushed up, meshed together mystically.

It is hard for me to understand men sometimes, to have a concept of them as an object, to understand their failure to communicate and the world they inhabit, their domain. The sense of their beliefs and mine differs profoundly. They can be monsters made of winter, coldly inspiring all kinds of aches and pains of the mental kind, cerebral but they can also be incredibly vulnerable. I ask myself, do I want to write. I can't remember when I wanted or started to write. When I received that inclination from the universe. I only knew that I had to write to save myself.

I don't remember when I remedied the thought of not dreaming with drinking. Alcoholism and crazy seemed inseparable and here is when the writing comes in, rescues me. The writing was always a useful exercise. I never learned to smile those early years in London, never believed I was a rose among the thorns. Perhaps all young women are supposed to think like that (that is what drives them, for the better part of my adult life it haunted me) and feel insecure in the bloom of their first love affair. I was not a flower, could not wrap my words around the tones of crisp English.

But I remember the tears. As a child, the back of my throat is a land of thirst. I knew that there was something else out there for me. Something besides the loneliness, the sadness and despair that I sometimes fell into, that became my child's mind-sanctuary. Dampness seeps into the lining of my coat. There are flecks of cloud in the blue sky. But is it enough to want desire? The faded grass under the leaves under my shoes. The faded grass under autumn leaves, Whitman's leaves of grass and the sacred contract that existed between human nature and nature.

The woman in the park she will not appear the same in a photograph as she will in memory. This Eve taken from Adam's rib who was a daughter doing what her mother did. Woman, the ethereal girl figure turning on a pedestal with her eye on the prize of love. I have my observations of them, these others, glorified futuristic poster girls for motherhood (who would in a few years' time settle down for life). They will live as they dream in their sleep and dream to live. And all my life I have wondered what do children communicate when they laugh?

Turkish slippers small enough for small frail bird feet, a gift from a friend. A draft of sunlight in the air burns bright. I am held, caught up in its grasp. Illness has touched the glinting, sharp parts of me. It is not the bag of bones why have you forsaken me, my skull, my frame, celestial nimble fingers, and patella. You centre of my being, nerve, every fibre of my being, brain, heart of mine, platelet, aorta, and corpuscle. Why this unfinished prophecy? And then it grew cold. It is as if cosmic force was holding all those clouds up together.

The world around me, its people, and the rich became wealthier, girls on the chorus line retired from the theatre life when they got married and everything around me moved forward. It got its talons in me and I never became that selfless kind of person I wanted to be. Darkness falls. At my core lies gravity. All my life I have wanted to be beautiful. I have everything else. I will never get married. It is all becoming a bit too much for me. A bit of losing my mind, my heavy head giving way. I can't keep lying. Keeping on and on with it. I must be honest. I must be truthful.

The unopened bottle of gin is there on the table. I must stop wasting my time. I must be brave and throw my head back and love, laugh in the face of adversity. I must stop wasting time. If I don't eat something I will disappear, that superimposed elusive part of me, the soul, the frightened part, and the physical and private body of the subconscious. I am becoming a non-entity. I can become used to the idea that I do not exist in the material world where the others meet. Men and woman of similar interests and backgrounds and who have common goals, that connects them to each other.

The morning air in my room is cold, heavy and still. So, I make way to the kitchen to smoke and although there are rats in the ceiling it is not all doom and gloom. The writing life has chosen me. Being happy is a unique state of mind. I can remember when I felt as if I was let loose on the world off the ship from Dominica to go to school in England. If only I knew then what I know now. London wasn't a distant place, it was a distant planet. The results can be electric when opposites attract. I could dance but I was not good enough, not graceful, less than the other girls.

I could act a little but then there was my West Indian accent. So, in the end it was decided that I was a terrible actress. I could not cry on command in class instead I started to laugh and to laugh and to laugh and that drew attention to myself. An artist works with materials at hand. Voice, the life force of the body, touch, hand movement, eye coordination, physical body, and the senses. What can be more precious than to be coloured by an auspicious space and when the abundant universe gives you wings?

To start from (childhood) and to transition it from a dream (to act on the stage) to a comfort zone (ending up in the chorus). Sharp, blistering, in a brutal dissolve came the comments when I was younger living in a house with other siblings, a father for a doctor and a mother who was always certain that I would fail if I set my heart on anything. Threads, connected by them govern us as we are by the books we read. I have a theory about

149

books. In the long run they will make you wiser but they will also make you cry, laugh, as wise as an owl.

Deep unhappiness can be challenging, that and learning to fight your battles. What many people don't realise is that egocentrism can be good for you up to a certain extent. Especially when you are given a stage, an expectant audience (a waiting one). When you are expected to shine brilliantly. It is egocentrism that wants, drives you and that gives you the ability to do well (ambition), expect a rousing applause, admiration, adoration, a standing ovation and to a certain extent love and acceptance and your abilities for being recognised for what they are.

Why is simply achieving happiness so hard? The negative ruins optimism. It ruins me for good. When I was younger, just a slip of a girl I wondered what having a backbone meant. My first prince did not love me. The most that he could give of himself was never quite enough. I wonder if the vegetarian restaurant that I frequented when I lived in London is still open. I ate the noodles and the soup it floated in heartily while watching the world go by. In those early years I was afraid of what was going to happen to me. Would I ever make it?

Would the lady in me ever come out, deserving of love, out of the hole, the void? This scared cat. I'm frightened of people who constantly tell you that they love you. Truth and beauty exist in a microcosm of things. Scientists will say it is atoms while I say I am a voyager and these are the sum of my parts. I believe in having interests and sticking to them. Having goals sometimes gives me light-headed feeling. Is that what I am really supposed to be here for? It makes me feel locked up, as if I have to have a witness or witnesses for everything that I do and envisage for my life.

I am always struck by how unsure I was by the cruel wonders, how filled with dangers the world was once. I did not become immune to it quickly. Do I have my upbringing to thank for that, I do not know. I feel lost sometimes when I stare at my reflection put out by unwanted visitors who go from door-to-door but I also feel pure of heart too. Men have done me no wrong, that charade is long gone. It is I who have been foolish and reckless with my own heart. You see why blame them. I miss the sea and the view from the top of the hill in Dominica.

The horses we had when I was growing up and when I got on that boat with my aunt that day to say goodbye to the world I grew up with forever I asked myself, what would I do in the world? Would I always be petrified, would warmth or the cold always strike me? I was always the curator of wish-fulfilment, dreams, an odd sort of museum where nothing fit because there was no culture too, and no sanctuary. There were moments in childhood when I despaired not having anyone to talk to. I remember the sadness that seemed to pale everything else in comparison.

I wanted to be happy but I didn't know why I wasn't a happy child. Why I never smiled like the other girls? I must have been too quiet. I must have been a mute. I must have been a dark mute with a dark soul, intense and always burning rough around the edges. No, I was never like the others. Not like my sisters with their lovely faces. I am not perfect. The perfect partner, co-conspirator, somebody's wife, the perfect daughter, and sister. In the end, it is just a not too long list of words. I never wanted to be alone.

I did not want to navigate the world flying solo with fingertips caressing maps. I will never forget Paris. I will never forget that I lost a child there and had a daughter. I am a mother, a writer and perhaps I wasn't a very good wife. Of course, I went back to Dominica but it wasn't the same. I was older and London had changed me for good. And perhaps it was the snow. I could never get used to the cold you know. The fires that always had to burn (what a waste of fuel) and I never really took care of myself in London the way I did after I got married for the first time, second and third.

After the third one I had money from the writing part of my life. Past is past but it was on a certain level it was never quite for me. I distilled it with my pen. Childhood wounded me. It still seeped into me somehow. Through my clothes and it got to the very heart of lonely me. At one point I must have looked like a bird, as thin as one. London wounded me, as did relationships, insights into the observations of other lonely people around me (I would watch them through the window at that vegetarian restaurant or sitting around me at the other tables). Tiredness that crept into my voice.

And then later my spirit. I was always ready to fly off the handle. If not now, when then. When will the world begin to become fascinating to my bright eyes, my bright intellect? When will I become fierce? I was an extra in the movies once but in the end it did not count for anything. It did not turn into anything. I was still the same old same boring me. And I cried. I would write into the night and I would cry when the rest of the world was sleeping and dreaming or coming out of a club into the empty London streets.

And in the morning when I woke up with the rest of the world I felt complete in a way I cannot fully come to grips with or make you understand. And now after all this time that has passed me by I feel ethereal. I have faced the angelic. It has taken me on and I have won. I am otherworldly by design. A design not of my own making. It has taken years. There is always a lesson in love even though you may think for now it is wounding your spirit. I was a bride. There I said it. There was never a word for this pent–up sadness that sometimes felt poetic.

I just knew I was on edge for some reason. I could never be the mistress of this bright and new force within me. Freedom like any consciousness- thinking awareness is a psychological construct. It is nothing more than that and if we think it is going to be more we are going to be sadly mistaken in the end or we will realise it too late. I was once a daughter then an orphan. I had the maternal instinct in my genes. It had to have been there. To know that kind of love and be on the receiving end of it anchored me. When I held my daughter in my arms I had never felt more at peace with myself.

My daughter's childhood songs, her many sweet, curious, inventive faces, the avalanche of presents I bestowed upon her on birthdays and Christmases. She had a father and that was also in a way a gift from me to her in a way even though the three of us couldn't be together, live together properly as a family. She was beautifully well brought up. When do routes become important? I fear only in later life. When you are too set in your ways. When my dear, you are old and think you are going crazy. What would it have been like to watch the Dominican sun setting in a sea lock-and-struggle? I would have given anything to see that tonight.

When you're in your bed at night with the thick covers pulled up around you and think you can hear something in the kitchen (when it is only a window you left open or a cupboard door that refuses even with the wind to bang shut). When you think that someone in the dark is out to get you, the bogeyman. I've journeyed. I've journeyed and have no regrets. The living keep on living while the dead turn to dust. Nothing really belongs to us. When we leave this world we take with us the possessions we arrived with – the lone self. Beyond evening's contours are the stars and even further out there is the moon.

And if I close my eyes, I can imagine being aware of nature or in touching the sky. I already said I was a bride. But I cannot remember if I felt passion that day. Of course, a ring did mean that now the two of us were now bonded together for life and that was with my first marriage. I had a passion for libraries that mildew smell, the ancient pages that almost seemed to wilt in your hand; those lose pages that seemed to have come undone. I had a passion for books, above all for notebooks I could scribble into my heart's content, and I always loved to read.

153

How do you shine if you are not guided by 'other hands' and by those 'elders' who had come before you in the world? Pain of the mind can be more devastating, felt more acutely than pain of the body. In my life there was always the baby, the sister, another sibling has taken my place and now overshadowed me in everything I did. How do you know you're alive? You find poetry, the way of the writer with all the cleansing rituals in the space of the writer, the table, the chair and water to drink, bread and cheese for a meal. And slowly I slip into a routine.

I get up in the morning. I smoke. I brush my dishevelled hair. I go for a long walk in the streets of London. I am not yet that famous writer who is now elderly, famous-enough to have a driver to take me around town and pick up parcels before he drops me off at home at a small cottage in Devonshire. And after my walk, I must write. I confess. I had a cat once. It was a proper Persian kitten but the people who looked after it didn't look after it really well. The poor thing died of neglect. And then I was sad again for a long time. You have to have a heart to get yourself attached to animals.

This is my voice, made of gossamer, tasting like the season's fruits or cauldron (take your pick). It is a voice that sounds like Keats, and I am offering it to the world. It is I who have closed doors on myself, escaped through the window that was left ajar and not the other way around.

And these are the notes from a writer's journal, my notes.

Shut the door. Shut out the quiet light. Tell yourself to swim away from the tigers with arms pillars of smoke. One day I will find myself in a forest without men, without huntsmen and warriors, nomads and ghosts that burn all hours of the day and night. One day I will dazzle and fizz like a champagne virgin (hiss like a cobra). I will laugh in all their faces. I will weave and thread stories, braid hair and dwell in possibility. My mother taught me that. White Knight you jewel. The bluish sky falls off you. I

154

prefer the word 'solitude' to 'loneliness'. White Knight you jewel of Hollywood. One day I will shut the door. One day I will shut out the quiet light. One day I will tell myself to swim away from the tigers. My tingling arms pillars of smoke.

What a pale and beautiful creature you are (you once were upon a time now worlds apart) but are you happy? You went on to paradise and wrote and wrote and wrote and won prizes and planted flags. My beautiful creature as cold as all things that come from the sea, the lover of love and picture of health. I have bits and pieces in memory of you of other peoples' keepsake stuff. The mouth so angelic and so grateful to be kissed and the eyes like dew. I knew at the end of it you would still have a soul to come home to. Alas, the same could not be said of me, dude in black, cowboy in black. To yearn for love, to live in that paradise again and again and again is a wish granted to a chosen few, the chosen ones and what happens to the others?

The others live to exist for their families, raising their children or for themselves, for their ego. If there is no love to feed you, nurture you, caress your tired or grief-stricken face at the end of the day then I imagine that there are people out there who sometimes feel as lost as I do. What can loneliness communicate to you? It is a lovely feeling. You're freer in a way than other people are. But who is there for you to talk to at the end of the day? People need companions. People need friends and family, loved ones and acquaintances. People need contact, closure, and relationships. There are people who build empires on these kinds of things. And then there are people who need, want, desire love as wide as river, as deep and beautiful as the Pacific.

And then there are people who turn their back on that and embrace a life guided by the pulse that tells them to be brave. And to turn their back on a world that calls them an Outsider, a loner, strange with strange ways of doing things, a strange way of thinking. And you just have to have the courage of your convictions if you are this sort of person. I am this sort of person. So weirdly out of sync with the rhythm of other women my age. So good I am at this thing, this sly-odd movement that I have won prizes for it. It feels like a bird's wing in spasm in the air. It feels like a rush of warm, sweet air into the beautiful red ribbons of your heart, a cry in the dark, a promise that you make to meet up with someone in heaven at a deathbed.

Someone dear and truly loved who has passed on from this world into the hereafter. What's eternity anyway? A more novel, adventurous dimension because it becomes lovely when you think of it in that way. Not meeting up with strangers but meeting up with familiar faces. The faces that you knew, loved and cherished since birth. They were people who were always a part of your world in one way or another. So I say one day we'll all meet in heaven. We'll make our way there from all of our other destinations that we 'lost' a little self, worth and identity in. Everybody is married in some way to his or her soul and every bit of our soul is intended for and to be hitched, hooked, stitched to God.

Whether you want to believe that or not is entirely up to you but to me it makes sense. I love the useful wonder in thinking that. And then there are those lukewarm questions that tug at the puppet strings of the heart. Not floating suspended by nothing but an existential breeze in the air, not drowning just there, behaving mysteriously as if they had all the right in the universe to be there. When I was in love, I wanted to know everything about him and nothing at the same time. Falling in love, head over heels, sweeping flaws under the carpet did not come with instructions. I did not know how to correct something I did wrong. Everything was new and pretty. To love someone since you were a child is a very long time.

Illusions, they do not come with flaws and they cannot love. They're too much in love with themselves. People do not ask, 'What were you like in the womb?' Men do not say with a great amount of insight, 'You seem to have been a fish with the spirit of a lioness even then.' They're answers for the volcano dreamer. The last battle was always touching and the solution for me is this. My sister and I had a conversation and it went something like this. We ended up not really saying anything at all like most of our conversations these days.

God can keep your soul. Let me bury you there in paradise. In no particular place in paradise. In your claustrophobic world where you were so cold. You, white knight death cutie on parade. It's the little deaths in pixels from childhood that is as nutritious and forgetful as dreaming. These days everything is crisper. Images are sharper and brighter.

(And now what about the men). Of course, the men are in secret code so they can never be discovered out. In a mirror I see a wife (always a fretful wife with screaming, crying babies). 'Poor babies,' I enjoyed saying and why didn't he love his beautiful wife more and why was I the chosen one. I couldn't really see why inexperience was so sexy. There is nothing barren about this man's ego. But his hands always felt cold. He had dark, dark hands; skin like velvet and even his eyes were dark. They were always so full of concern for me. I pretended it was a wonder. Living your life and moving forward is the easy part. It is the forgetting that is the hardest.

I can put a face to a name, city, and occupation. I remember. It is all in the details.

I don't want to meet these men in heaven or in any place else. The men with all that sadness, rage and perfect-wonder in their eyes. All their faces look the same to me and after all this time I did not step back from the picture and say I forgive this and I forget that. They look at me as if to say, 'You too had a role in this. A part to play in all that drama.' The drama felt quite useless to me on the one hand and like jazz on the other. 'You're quite mad, you know.' One man told me but he couldn't exactly look me in the eye. So, I bravely posed in mask after mask after mask. Another man preferred 'the girl'. Well, that was his thing. He didn't want to be educated, intelligent or smart. He didn't want cute. He wanted 'the girl'.

He wanted a pure, angelic face in beautiful clothes. He wanted obedience. He wanted to be put on a pedestal and worshipped. And so I did all that. I couldn't quite understand why because I could make conversation but he never wanted to talk and understand how claustrophobic I felt sometimes just being in his presence. It felt completely otherworldly to me. These things called love or rather, 'the affair'. It didn't exactly feel like romance to me. No, there was nothing romantic about it. I feel a great deal of shame because I did not listen to my heart. A heart that was telling me his wife meant a great deal more to him than I did and even on a certain primaeval level his wife's body meant a great deal more to him. She had given him children.

And he had built the house they all lived in (the one, big, happy and boisterous family). But since this is my secret diary it is just between you and me and nobody else has to know especially my father. I don't want him to think differently about me and the life I chose to give or take a few years ago because I am not that person anymore. And I don't believe that time heals. When people say that it is as if there's something specific to time. There's nothing specific about time and even clarity doesn't even figure into it. I can ask my ancestors why I've never been lucky in love. Why I've failed so dismally in that department (much too much of a daddy's girl)?

I can say I will never give my heart away again but I don't believe that.

I usually fall in love up to three times a day.

I was just starting to feel hungry. And when I am hungry I have my breakfast, usually toast with a smidgen of butter (from a brick that's been standing out on the kitchen table or counter since the following night) or margarine. And I make myself some tea. Just toast (brown bread toasted in the oven like in the old days and I smile when I think to myself that I am from the old days now). I wake up earlier and earlier and go to bed later and later. It feels good to be thirty-two. I didn't feel it (old, stale, as if I was coming into a rut, the state of the nation, the world my generation found themselves in) when it was my birthday but now that the next one is around the corner I am feeling it.

It feels like too much effort this morning to make an egg, boiled, fried, or scrambled into bits. So, I'll have my toast with jam this morning. I think of him and every day it doesn't hurt less, it hurts more. I've given up on humanity. What I see on the news or the little I read in the newspapers terrifies me. It scares me half to death. Children raping children (aren't they just babies), the desolation of poverty and how it isolates people from the mainstream of society. What is relevant to me in society is not relevant to the media. They write what sells and it is usually salacious material. Here today, gone tomorrow or the next week until it comes back as an update or haunts you when you least expect it.

It is funny how the mind can play tricks on you especially when you're over thirty, reaching that point of middle age. The news often pins down the status of refugees, painting the women with their children, food aid flown in from abroad, white tent after white tent in a field of white tents and again there are stories of rape and mutilation. It never seems to end. We are capable of many, many things. God can keep your soul and man will take and take everything else. I never thought of myself as a fierce person as a child. I was an introvert. I never thought of my mother as a bully although she could be quite fierce. When I was in London I hid all my diaries at the bottom of my suitcase and forgot about them.

In London, I would meet a man. We would eat noodles at a restaurant or go out for a drink. In Paris life was different. When I would meet a man there we would go out for a drink at a café. The lifestyle in Paris was like that. Drinking sparkling wine into the early hours of the morning. I would become a different person. I liked myself more. When I was with a man I told myself this was it. This is what passion felt like when I was in his arms. This was love, beauty and when it ended, when we went our separate ways there were days when I felt I was going out of my mind. The loneliness, the fear that I would never have that again made me turn to writing. I would open up the black scribbler.

I would sit and think to myself isn't that the most perfect word in the universe. In the middle of the night in my stockinged feet I would just glance out of my window and watch the world go by, trembling, chilled to the bone, drinking milk from a chipped mug. And I would write and write and write. It would simply pour out of me like rain from the sky while I would sit in my room. And so a book would turn into the pages of books, a stream of thought would lead to a threshold. I could now connect threads from my past to my present. I could still remember the ice house of my childhood, aunts, visitors to the house, voices, a mother who did not have the heart, the slightest idea, nor the inclination to love me. She could murder chickens though.

Strangle them by their necks. In a way she strangled me too. Perhaps when life is hard for women when they are girls who always have to compete for the love of their father that kind of intent is simply woven into their consciousness. Stars. Stars. I never see them in London but the night sky in Paris is full of them. I wonder how I will look in middle age when beauty and appeal and the sex drive, that impulse when a man is drawn to woman will fade. Life is poetry, my childhood in Dominica and women with their ammunition and their apparel. I never thought of other women as being in competition with me for the approval of men until the end of my first love affair. And then there was the poetry in my twenties. It cut me deep from skin to bone. I could feel it you know. There was nothing dysfunctional about the cut. Only I felt its power keenly, its voice, the chains and links of the voids therein. It stated wish fulfilment, commentary on modern issues and I felt it intensely at night when the world around me was asleep, when I felt drowsy or secretly despair at the situations and conflict I found myself in. Sometimes I even hated myself because I knew with some finality now that I had created the world I lived in now. There was no going back. Childhood, whatever state of mind, flux I had created then and now was over in a strong and futile sense. I could never get it back (whatever normal was). Normal was a word everyone used.

It was a word everyone around me, even my family believed in. It was a word that depressed me. Was I a lady? I who was so ignorant of many things, that had so few belongings, not even a tiny flat or house with two bedrooms to my name, furniture that I could move and place in rooms as I pleased. Had I ever really been in love and loved? I believed that secrets should never be told. But I told my first husband everything. I wanted to believe that he loved me completely, that the past didn't matter. Back and forth I would go every night writing effortlessly in my black notebook. The past, history came with such ease. In this day and age the woman I had become was called a non-conformist.

The norm was to get married before you were thirty and have children, a house, housekeeper, maids, a linen cupboard, have holidays, go camping, to the seaside. Of course, I thought I would and could have all these things. I would have worked for it but shock and horror it did not come my way. I was left behind while others stronger than I was took that shot at the big time. I shook it, writing all my secrets down (the parts of me that just did not fit in this life, this city). I shook it off my chest like a fish hooked on a fisherman's line shook the breeze and seawater off its scales, and fins and back. Sometimes I thought to myself, 'Jean, you're missing out. You're missing out on life.'

Sometimes I would say to myself, 'What if you'd just let yourself go a little? Talk a little, make a little conversation, be brave, braver, and confident like those mannequins in the window that you passed today with their chins up.' I thought I would only become illuminated as a woman when he, the man in my life stroked my cheek, my palm, my bottom lip, my head and it would always come with a rush of this feeling to my head. He is so pale and beautiful, so fragile and delicate, like a flower in the winter light. The hush of silence in the room is as soft as feathers. His breath is as fresh as water. His soul is perfect but he doesn't know this yet. I imagine it's a feeling he will only experience with his children and his future wife.

Now he is a work in progress, caught between two worlds and enjoying the view. It is as pure as white-hot chemistry. His eyes are wet and dreamy. His hands and his fingertips are not delicate. They bruise the wasteland of my face easily. When I was away from him the world around me became cold. It felt like a feast of winter all around me.

A heavy glow, inviting look, a picture of innocence colours your look of the world, of how to be loved. Tonight, I am an empress of cool in my dress and for a time now there has been no new money for new dresses. It hurts so much when he touches me on my arm when he puts his arm around my shoulder I shudder. I can sometimes feel the chill wrapped in his embrace. His fingertips burn my skin, my lips. The only thing that soothes me is his kisses, his presence and the fact that now in the bedroom we are equal. Now submission, role-play, pain and pleasure are open to interpretation. He is gentle around me tonight, he is not angry, emotional or abusive, hurling abuse, screaming at me. His day must have gone reasonably well.

This relationship doesn't heal anything in my past; bring emotional closure to the abuse I suffered in my childhood. It only serves to encase my newfound promiscuous behaviour in Technicolor in a bubble, in a grandiose time warp. I can't make him love me. Yet he is just as much impossible to love with his own mood swings as I am. I am always forgiving of his artistic temperament. I ask myself what is his heart, his soul trying to express. He's just as wounded as me. Comfort me, hold me just a while longer but he doesn't make eye contact with me and speak to me. After making love I am as empty as a drum. I watch him sleep and feel fiercely protective over him. No love lost, only my innocence.

Before I was invincible, and now in his arms, I am fragile and delicate. From far away I hear myself say, 'Say something funny. Make me laugh.' He smiles, looks at me as if to say, 'I am not in love with you' but I don't care. For now, he is all mine. He belongs to me. His body, his jokes, the smell of his aftershave, his stories, his eyes, his lips so soft and delicate and bruising all at once. He is bitter. He is sweet. He does not believe in me, he does not believe me when I say that I love him. In my heart I say, I'll take you just the way you are, you maladjusted, maladroit, abusive, abused child from one abused, damaged and neglected child to another. He can see me and that is enough for me.

I wash his back in circles, making ripples in the water with the palm of my hand, talking in circles but he doesn't say anything meaningful back. I know he's just using me, humiliating me and causing a future exposure to trauma. I don't know any better, anything else, any other life. What is the reward, what is the payoff? Even when he humiliates me, he is still looking at me, working miracles on me. I have become an addict. It doesn't matter whether or not he speaks to me with contempt. I am convinced I have nothing without him. I am convinced I am nothing without him. Look at me, rescue me, save me; but the lost boys with vacant eyes and vague promises never do.

They leave me feeling haunted and blue with ice water running through my veins. They never smile at you until you smile on the outside. If I am quiet it's because of the urgency in his voice, his breathing, his movements (himhimhim). Shame was a word I heard often when I was a weak child with a raving mother who often taunted me. And in this ice house there was no beauty, prettiness, loveliness, only grief, weariness, and a cry in the dark. I could not be alone and feel that kind of fire. And at that time in my life and in all the faces I saw around me all I saw and heard was, 'I do not, I do not, I do not love you.' And so order was spoiled and chaos ensued. I became frantic and believed that Lolita's passage had set my own.

I kept my heart in a jar and my head in the sand. Everything happened so fast that I had no control over the pressure, the tightness of the close-knit and newly formed friendships, the disturbance, and the disturbances. I felt I could no longer live in a world that was not accepting of me. So I had to create a character in a storybook, a fairy tale to be loved, a glutton for punishment. For me, he would bruise me to the bone, to my psyche. I'm a dazzling insomniac. Even my silent screaming when I am falling apart is dazzling with my every waking thought and living moment. I brought submission to the table. I had solitude on my side. He had a kind of self-leadership about him then. I was alive even in those empty moments.

I learnt to say if you feel like it then love me, if you don't then don't. I began to see his, my, our rituals as crucial turning points in the relationship. I could not bear being alone, being left alone.

Poetry continued in my thirties (there's room now for a view)

The discovery of hearts in jars

There are things

I will never forget

The art of making war

Instead of peace

How it nurtured luminous me

Without me knowing

That time was slipping away

In one lifetime

There can be many passions

That can be part of your heart

That tells you to have courage

The headline read, 'Let's stop the persecution'. It could have been something I had written, perhaps a letter to the editor. I saw a flash, a slap against a face across the breakfast table and my sister gave a shout and began to cry. I remember washing my hair in a woman's salon and reading about the virgin lover in Nabokov's Lolita. My fingers holding onto the spine of the book, bookmarking the last page I read. The girl sitting next to me at the basin had doll eyes. They were brown with gold, golden flecks in them and so I began to learn what any woman would do for vanity in high school. As a child, I grew up in a house made of brightness, made up of bright things. Tough love was a shiny bullet flying through the air. The surfaces were conservative, tense yet tidal, emotions running high, the collection of them and those experiences hard. And then I began to long for the weight of the meditative hush in leaves. It was the only thing that brought me peace of mind and that froze both joy and deception in their tracks. I wanted to be the sensible child taking the separation or divorce pretty well. I wanted to tell my mother that she hurt the people who loved her the most.

Where the woman of the world is illumined

The unseen is eternal

The world is not my home

I am here on earth for a little while

I have left childhood behind

One day I will let go

Of everything that intoxicated

Me before

What orientated me?

Before will come to an end

This is the sound of one voice

Speaking to me

But he, my father does not give of himself effortlessly or consistently. There were often closed doors. They would bang shut and it could be heard in all the rooms. It could even reach children who were supposed to be asleep, their ears. It couldn't have been that serious. I heard my mother laughing. She sounded free. Free in the sense that she was a young girl again without any limitations being placed on her. The limitations of a family and a husband and especially work. My mother and sister had the personality of a volcano. All I could taste was rain, pretend that I was dead in the sea whenever, wherever I heard a shriek of excitement on the beach from other children building castles. I imagined auras while their mothers dried their hair with a towel and gave them money, pressed silver coins in their hand for ice cream or for something cold to drink. Other children would parade and dance in front of their mother's. I wanted to be left alone. I was always a child on the verge of a nervous breakdown. As a young woman, I wanted my gracious, appreciative heart to locate others.

Through the eyes of the child

For all my life

You've painted me

In journals

Inside my head

There's a silent sea

A quiet town setting

Poetry in a scrapbook

An exquisite identity

I am a poet

In a pot in bloom

Before being launched into space

The art was not to fall like the virgin lover in Nabokov's Lolita. But fall I did. It was always cold where I was. It was not my dream to be endeavoured with literary pursuits from a young age. Children do not have the mental faculty to wish fear away in an instant. Children are just brave. They just seem to have that cosmic life force. I don't think I was a brave child. I wanted to be a volcano but I just didn't have that in me. And when I grew up into a young woman, into a writer, that oppressive feeling that I had to be emancipated in some or all the way never left me. It stayed with me at my side. It was my doppelganger. And as I became a vibrant type of person and my thoughts more and more vivid I could see all the beauty in the world around me except in me. All I could understand was people and write about them and me observing them. Playing dead in the water, in the end, had served me well and had taken me to new heights and had fostered an unseen intelligence. My father did everything but talk. Meanwhile, I pulled out the entire minimum stops and shortcuts.

And so I come

To the end of violence

He never said please

He never said thank you

He touched the nerve centre

Of all my despair and madness

And perhaps that was the end

Of joy in my life

The beginning of silence

In the background of rooms

When I began

To flirt with the temptations

Of this world

Purpose is life. The war inside my mind is often a war of nerves, a crowded house. It leaves me with a feeling of being locked up inside a box, Pandora's Box. There's place for stigma and being, the unbearable in there as well. Living in a fog-like consciousness, always watching the clock, that round island made up of numbers. So, I had to discover that the universe promises the human condition two things: mortality and eternity. Depression doesn't come with a vision of the world. It comes with its own canvas, blank and its own personal mission, do or die, go beyond yonder. The proof of depression is something absurdly supernatural, that there is something greater than you are even if it is a calling and a gift in your blood. You need to learn how to fly, the machinations of your consciousness 'caught by the river' by the river exploding into life in front of your eyes. Sometimes the story begins at the end or with flashbacks with dramatic effect moving forwards and backwards. It is blood that is thicker than water, than family bloodlines or the phoenix rising from ashes.

Head against the brick and stone of depression is often a permanent protest. When I began to write poetry I left space for interpretation, for kindred spirits and soul mates, even for ghosts. It is brutal, dissolves, deranges, distorts and it drums this into you. It has such a presence, pain, depression, melancholia standing at attention. Poetry became my goal (the force of my reality, the reality I lived in) and my life. It became my desire that existed in both the spirit of place of darkness and light. It became the psychosomatic root of my cognitive thinking and my self-help. When you're depressed you keep your thoughts and reflections to yourself. They're more often than not charged with electricity, electricity that is not easy to shield yourself from like the eye of the sun. 'Come back to bed.' Your body says. Your eyes are vacant hinting at the spark and the glow of the displeasure of ill health, old wounds and escape. You feel naked as if you've been abandoned in the dark, the pitch black and thrown to the wolves. I make lists of things that trouble me when I feel depressed. Any female writer would write what she feels destination anywhere in an upside-down world.

Nothing fades away except the material world and the physical body. And so I found myself in the city of cities, bereft, sinking my teeth into the polished floors of the library, the archives, the newspapers, textbooks, novels and biographies, anything that I could get my hands on and read. I was a film student marching across asphalt and green armed with books and not so often an engaging intellect. If only people were more like me, I wondered. If only people were not so mediocre. If only the other students did not spend their time drinking so much, not understanding me, sharing cigarettes. And then there was the woman with a feather in her hair, a modern-day witch. Her skin dark and ashy she would dance madly with rhythm in the halls of the ward in the hospital with feathers in her hair. I could not understand her, the mechanism, that shift within her brain, whatever was in her head, that swift shift in the chains of her consciousness like leaves against grass, Whitman's Leaves of Grass, Lewis Hyde's The Gift. It was here that I discovered Goethe. All I could think to myself was that this was madness and that madness could be as magnificent as the highs of euphoria.

Nothing unique but as weeks went by it didn't seem to fade away into the comfort blanket world of inhibitory drugs and prescribed medication and that beautiful Lithium. I could only face the world with the psychology I gleaned from my reading, delving deep into the ghostly facets and facts of the unstable planet of illness and mental illness. I grew excited by the potential that lay ahead of me, in the distant future. It was always hours away. All I had to do was built on the edges of a dream.

When I think of that time before my life began once more in search of a fabulous road, I seemed to live in a nation in ruins in that hospital, filled with ruined people, and lives that were intensely fragile. Their sadness seeped into me like stains in the peeling wallpaper at the Salvation Army. I needed to feel alive and I could only feel alive when I was witnessing the pain of other souls and when I could tell and see how the world put pressure on them to excel. I began to live in books and on the plateaus and landscapes it offered me. I needed to picture a life without the cool order and routine of student nurses hovering, staring at a television's snow. For now, I needed that but I needed the world too.

Dark, dark, dark and just like that it was gone. I am the way I am because of my mother, other women, my father, aunts and the hidden meaning in responsibility. I have felt devastation all my life, loss, people simply passing through my life going from one place to the next and I have found that words are the easy part. The outside world doesn't inform anything that you say or do when you are living with ghosts that you're waiting to be cured of. His eyes were a sea of green glass and his hair was long and dark. We could talk for hours sitting on the grass. I would stare into his eyes and that glass would chip away at the fragments of my heart. I even found time to fall in love and out of hate with my soul (what is does it mean to have a soul) and with the being of myself. I found I could reconstruct the material, make it emotive, and make it glad. I wanted to bring my family back together again. I wanted to heal what was broken. All I saw around me were broken people, shattered people, people in recovery under daily observation and I was one of them. I felt as if there was some part of me that didn't belong to the world. Yonder, unbearable light, madness, illness, scar tissue, a heavy kind of woundedness can do that to you.

And what are women truly at heart if the writers are the thinkers. Poets are dreamers and being conscious of their dreams they are conscious of the guts they have to live in this damned-if-they-do, damned-if-they-don't-world. We have to start somewhere I reckon, all women do. We are the ones who have to come up with a blank emotionally intuitive and spiritual slate before our written words become imprinted on an audience, a reader, a woman, a man or a child. Before we burn away into nothingness, before we escape, and before truth stares us down in the face. Awareness and the grit in our souls always come with nurturing and until there's an unbearable lightness in our awareness, a turn of the switch to develop this spirit in others.

Our writing (female writing) only becomes more successful when we inspire others to gravitate towards greatness. From a youth's pure and angelic roots to being a walking mass of contradictions as they grow, to their bones, the consciousness of a movement has begun across the female nation reaching converging lines bordering on the universal. Writers' psyches cannot survive in dysfunction without the pictures of our external reality growing cold and dim as they fill inner space, marking turning points in time, in the flesh of history books. This is my message to the youth of the world. Pay attention to your dreams. The light in all of you is like a volcano. It can melt the heart of stone.

Perhaps one of the loneliest experiences in the whole world is this, writing. I say this because on the surface I feel I can make it look effortless (there is a transference, a catalyst that I can't explain, can't put my finger on) while inside the vision we have this surface that if looks could kill it could kill. I've realised through my long walks that the woman who is secure in her home is the woman who has married, who has those children, who cooks those breakfasts and steaks, maintains a household, is the lady of the house. She is the madam who orders the kind of fish her husband likes to have. She puts honey and lemon in her tea, serves it like that when guests come to her house.

Other women her age, other women with the same interests she has, who have the same number of children that she has. She does not have to put her coat on, her scarf, and her hat and open the door and walk out into the world a leper, yes, I say a leper because she is rejected wherever she goes. She is the Outsider, the loner, isolated. Nowhere is there a paradise for her. There are norms and values. What are the norms and values of a single woman (note I did not say the single 'lady')? A single woman is a burden to her family if she is unemployed. If she does not have any skills and her loveliness fades away swiftly. Nobody wants to have anything to do with her. They do not want to talk to her, converse with her because she does not have any talents.

If she had they've already convinced themselves of this fact that she would've been married long ago, off their hands. She will never find herself in a field of love. Instead, she will imagine what it would be like. She would imagine the atomic illusion of it. And she will know deep in her heart that she will be a girl for the rest of her life, a being who will never be swept off her feet by a masculine swagger. She would never understand what the words 'flirt', 'flirting' meant. She would remain detached from the world her cousins now inhabit, tangled in obsession. Men like to eat meat and she will remember meals she had with a man once or twice. How he licked the fat off his lips and drank his wine and how kind he was to her like her father was and when she thought of that she would always think of Dominica.

Is there anything else you would like, maybe a dessert, something sweet, a treat to end our meeting like this?

You know it's not always going to be this way.

I want you to remember me like this always, and that we were happy and friendly and our parting was amicable. Let us part as friends. Smile, I know you can.

I have a present for you. It isn't wrapped though, forgive me. I painted it myself. It's a landscape. It's pretty isn't it? I'm thinking of buying a house there. You've never been to the country before, have you? It's beautiful and quiet. Business is business but you have to live somewhere too, you know. You have to live.

But I didn't know. I didn't know how to live, how to ask, 'Are you happy now?' All I seemed to say over and over again was, 'Are you happy now, Jean? Is this what you wanted, or was it a manifesto of loneliness and despair that I had been searching for all of my life since childhood?' All I knew was hotel room after hotel room, meetings there, situations there. I wanted to be filled bit by bit with love and empathy for other people who seemed to find themselves in the same situation I was in. They were lost. I was lost. I was scared to find out that I had no substance. I was baffled by the life around me and the lives people were living. It was as if they were telling me I was the fraud, the fake, and the poser.

I still don't know how it came about, the writing part of me that bit. Now when I come to my younger sister she is half otherworldly, half superimposed in reality. Now she is made of substance. God, why am I not? Why? So here I am? Why?

I don't know what love is, what love is made of, why I am out of touch with that reality and I've been out of touch with it for a long time. So here I am in London where the lights aren't as bright as they are in Paris and in my dreams I was in Dominica. It was always playing at the back of my mind. There was nothing European about me although I had travelled on the continent. A man gave me advice once. I didn't take it. Oh, I pretend to listen and it's alright for them to know that I am just pretending too while they pretend to care about me.

What are you thinking about in that intelligent little head of yours Jean? I don't think you need saving. I think you're fierce enough to understand your circumstances, to grapple with the future that lies ahead of you, to take it on. Not many women can do that. Are you lonely? Even I get lonely sometimes. Sometimes even when I'm surrounded by other people truly living. What does it mean to truly live? Does it mean to be happy, and content, the weight of a ravaged country or mountain off your back? Money does not make anyone happy. It can make you, give you a certain

174

sense of power and control over other people but coming back to you, pet; you give me that impression that all 'little Jean' had known in a way her whole life was suffering.

It is a reality I can't bear to face, to face this existence, this depression, this illness. You might think I'm brave but I don't think I'm brave. There is nothing heroic about miserable me I'm afraid. I sought out male companions who were pure of heart and failed miserably at that too. While leaves curled up (I too curled up in my bed at night), shrivelled up (my soul shrivelled up), winter danced away and seasons passed, turned into the loving of summertime I took to the streets again and little cafes. I casually observed the ballad of the human race around me and the wonder of loneliness. It took guts to live and I was so meek, so weak, mousy. I did not know how to live. Nobody had taught me anything about that.

I had to steal it the best way I knew how. By using my brain as a catalyst and by filling black notebooks with the winters, the breath of the wilderness, the wild of life, the Technicolor of poppies in a field, drops of rain on a drab coat, shoes that looked a bit worse for wear. I wanted to remember Dominica (my choice). Not the suffering but the lavishness of the books I stuck my nose in the library when I was a child. It made me feel better. I too had a right to live in this world. You, anyone, could not take that away from me. I was not a ghost although I moved like one through the streets. I have finally decided what my gift was to this world. Sacrifice. I am still here. Magnificently I am still all here.

The unbearable light in having a bright conversation, sharp, bright, intuitive eyes with insight into the world around sensitive me. I need a drink, badly, to forget all about yesterday. I'm pensive (don't give a damn about this maddening hell that seems to cavort beautifully, helplessly around me. I drown in its echo, its phenomena.) Am I cultured? Am I educated? I always wanted to be. I wanted to be a woman who is secure in her own home. I wanted to be a brutal thinker, a woman who has not been initiated into the sexual impulse (the wonder of a kiss, the virgin seed awakening to consciousness in a touch, love, beating heart, romantic interlude) at an early stage of her development. Poor me, hey.

I don't think my mother ever knew how much she really hurt me. I think when I first became aware of that I became less trusting of the world around me. I became detached from it in a sense and there I was thrust into a state of imbalance. I could no longer feel the flux of equilibrium, fisherman's thievery, the glint of the silver skin of the fin of the fish. Love stories come from that place, the land of immortals. They truly last forever but love affairs are another equation, another seam, hemmed in by mirth, priorities and cons. They're inelegant. A love affair drifts. You can't read its palm. It has a noose tied around its neck. It's loosed into the world like it has been there forever. It's just an obsession. It is just an obsession in an open love field.

I met someone once. He smelled like the earth. His hands were rough. He wore a mask and I had one too but it didn't matter. It didn't matter that we couldn't define the boundaries of the relationship. He made me feel as if I could do anything, be anything, feel alive. It was as if I had just come into being, you know. And when it rained, I didn't feel the rain. When I was away from him the world no longer felt uninviting and cold, grave and condescending. I could look people in the eye because now I too was a possession. The dark no longer made a cripple out of me. It no longer burned me, that giant. I could close my eyes and fast forward to a time that I looked forward to. I no longer said, 'What is love anyway? It means nothing to me.'

I would sit across from him at a table at a restaurant (he would order and he'd be in charge) and he would say things that would fill me with delight, with bliss, something would just shift inside of me. I would no longer be a girl; I would become a woman, a fashionable lady. I would sample everything on my plate. I would warm to him. The days when I felt persecuted by sitting idle while the world would go by would be long gone. He would colour my life now. He would lecture me not my subconscious, and not the inner spaces of my mind. I'd think to myself that now I have no more adversaries. Now I have my revenge. I only have to compete with other women who are in my position. My lonely days were over (not completely.) There was a part of me that knew that there would be a new area where desolation would await me. I would be hungry for more shades of energy, power, and love. As soon as the person or people in the next room or downstairs moved out, someone new would move in.

Sylvia and Ted

Sylvia and Ted

'In fact, you're saying that I'm about to 'dig my own grave' again, so here goes.' She said with a small, knowing smile.

'Shouting is your drug, Sylvia, not mine. You're just doing this to test my loyalty to you.' He threw his hands up in despair.

'You've tested my love every day of this marriage.' She yelled.

'I live for you and those two children. They're my blood.' He yelled back.

'You want to leave me. I can't cope. I won't. I won't be alone.' She pouted and sulked.

'Nobody's asking you to go out on your own, to be by yourself and be a single mother to two small children. You're putting words in my mouth.' He counterattacked.

'Liar, don't deny you've ever thought that it would be easier on both of us if you did.'

'I never betrayed you, Sylvia. I never had an affair.'

Journal entry

The page frees me in a sense, in a way I can't describe. I write and that's my life. I am a mother and a wife and a lover and a poet and I feel that is also just a part of my life. Sometimes the two meet and sometimes they don't. Sphere upon sphere upon another sphere. Poetry is a god to me. When I write I am a woman on her own. Reality is out of the picture and it doesn't seem to count for anything really. It's never enough for me. I stand and watch the busyness of life, observing nature and most of all human nature and I slowly empty out. It's a useful exercise kind of like transcendental meditation. I know nothing about it. It's just something I read as a girl in a book long ago when I was at college and at the time it was just too much for me to handle. The thought of going out of myself made me go numb and cold. It gave me the shivers. If I was alone I would go mad with grief and rage and I would be that girl again.

Sylvia and Ted

'Sylvia, I'm here now, that should count for something.'

'Betrayer. I don't want you here. We don't want you here. Go to that brazen woman. Declare your love for her. Hold onto her not me. She's sane and attractive. Is she kind? She tolerates you. She's got everything going for her. Go and have your love affair. I hope it inspires you. No, I hope she inspires you to greater heights.'

'I regard you, Sylvia, as the most important person in my life. You are a nurturer and caregiver to my children, you are my wife, my life, my mate, my life partner. Why can't you see that?'

'Why can't you see that I'm not blind or stupid? I have eyes. I can see. Do you think I don't have the faith to know that maybe this is not going to work out happily ever after? I know you've been keeping secrets from me. Ted, a woman knows everything.'

Journal entry

I think I've been supportive. I've been encouraging. All I see are constellations in words and it is driving me sweetly out of my mind. I am the rabbit in Wonderland and there I go down that hole. There are people out there who have peace around them all the time. Why can't I be one of those people? Life is a cruel trick. I want to escape from my reality. Women don't set out to alienate men. It's not their lot in life. Men and women are supposed to get along so they can walk down that sunny road, settle down and marry and have those kids and start the modern family. Sylvia and Ted are just complex, endlessly searching particles bumping into each other for clarity like oil and water, like acid rain. Now we, the both of this 'us' that he keeps on talking about have this one thing in common and that is poetry and the goal was for us to work together but now it is working against us. I never dreamed that this would be kismet.

Sylvia and Ted

'I don't want to talk to you anymore. I hate you. Look what you've done. You've made me hate you. You've turned me into a scorned woman. I'm bitter and cold. You're distant. You are so distant from me and you don't even know it. Don't even try to explain your way out of this. I saw the way you looked at her. The way she looked at you. It was in the way you spoke to each other, leaned in when the other one was talking. You're driving me up brick walls and down brick walls and all the while I am hitting my head against them. It hurts. It hurts. It hurts. I have this pounding headache from beating my pretty little blonde head against them.'

'Sylvia, Sylvia, Sylvia. Listen to me. We can fix this. I can make 'us' right again.'

'There is nothing, nothing in this world that you can do to bring the two of us back to where we came from, that perfect moment, that perfect start. You're such a coward.'

Journal entry

Last night I was electric. I told him where to get off and come hell or high water I am going to stick to it. So sticking to my guns, that's me. I put the universe under observation. To be a wonder, I sometimes long for that. To sparkle, to vibrate, to feel that there's enough in the world, to bask in the revelation that there's an abundance healing the world of all its iniquities through ritual, that there's healing across family bloodlines. I long to be so innocent and pure and that I would have no knowledge of the raw energy of blood and guts in writing poetry. I go inside. Inside the deepness, the thoroughfare of the sense and sensibility of every female poet and what do I find there wherever I look. Boxes that are locked and keys that need to be found, a heart that needs to be connected to the material, the physical part of the universe to view even the light and dark battling it out.

Sylvia and Ted

'Do you need more clarity than this? Do you really need another explanation? Do you want the truth? I want out of this mess, this relationship and this marriage, Ted. There is no more 'us'. There isn't a future for 'us'. Who is this 'us' you keep on talking about?'

'You don't have to scream. I can hear you perfectly. Sylvia, be reasonable, be sensible.'

'I'm sensible to the moon and back, reasonable until I'm all worn out with the very act of it. All I do is live for you, respond to your every thought and breath and movement. How agile you are Ted, no, you're really an animal, to escape and not to escape, through your work and your lectures and other women. Your hunger inflames me. Don't tell me that there have never been other women.'

Journal entry

Poetry has become my life work, my death of self, a force to be reckoned with steely-eyed determination, my love, my creative impulse and passion. It is the fruit of my spirit and the way of my soul. I have found the world, worlds really that exist in my consciousness, that state I can only reach when I am very still and quiet. The state I could reach when I was young. You only have that kind of inclination when you are young and you don't live in a constant state of denial of fear and the ego and insecurity. So I have found consciousness, that clear and fluid stream of thought that tends to linger. The heavenly creation of a dream does not. And when you wake up in the morning there is action and vision and doing your ablutions, brushing the curls out of your hair, there's a sense of orderliness in the routine. There is always something human. I must have courage now. This is not my first hurt.

Sylvia and Ted

'Just say it. Go ahead. I am waiting for you to say it. There, say those words that will shield you from this manic rage, this episode, episode after episode. Sylvia, don't let's argue, don't let's fight in front of the children.'

'You can cut through this tension with a knife. You're the knife in this equation, Ted and you're cutting my heart into little, tiny pieces until there's nothing left of the love and respect I felt for you when I first met you. Presently I feel nothing but pity for you.'

'I think you're making yourself sick with worry and disgust. There's no need for this unpleasantness.'

'Do you know how much I crave your honesty?'

'You want everything from me.'

'Is that asking too much? Poor Ted. My expectations of you are too high. I'm disappointed in you.'

Journal entry

I see myself as a poet and a female writer second. There's no contest. All of life is feeding ghosts that came before and after, running on your own personal velocity, the flow of poetic motion, a writer saying, 'I need an ending to this' blasting through his or her dream. Inside the mind/vision of a poet means going into the black and that there are always two possibilities within reach, life or death, feeding the gods of beasts or feeling ghosts near your fingertips, depression or feeling that you're more normal, stable than the next person. I think I have found my ending. Once you are there you're running, running with scissors (and didn't even know it). For writers all of life is childhood continued. As a writer, now is the time of my life. Sylvia writes every day, that is the purest sum of parts of a writer. Don't edit. Don't censor yourself. Before you show 'the work' to anyone else, journal with intent.

Sylvia and Ted

'The woman I knew, the woman I got married to was a big, beautiful dreamer with wisdom, life experiences, ideas filling up space and void, heart and mind, the battlefield of emptiness, valley and black sea of the sorrow. The woman I married also had a desolate feeling of loneliness and perhaps in some way I was attracted to that.'

'You've hurt me so much. I don't think I can ever forgive you for this.'

'You said once that I make you happy. Sylvia, look at me when I talk to you. We had that connection when I first met you. You're not alone, Sylvia. I said I would protect you.'

'No, I have to shield myself from you, from all your airs and your charisma and your swagger. You don't make me feel safe anymore. I even believe that I don't love you anymore. I am not in love with Ted Hughes and I can scream it from the rooftops.'

Journal entry

Loss is a hard fall. You're standing and then the world becomes something of a hallucination. Writing no longer is a task for me. Feeling broken is a splendiferous stain. Held up to the world it is my main inspiration. It packs it in, crosses thresholds, divides, and flaunts, what it isn't is anonymous. In my writing I don't have to don a mask and mask my pain. I don't have to filter my moods and then I turn to my reflection and say, 'Bravo, Sylvia. You've done the impossible. Bravo.' Perhaps it is true. I am behaving like a spoilt, coddled child. But if I take him back what does that say about me, all my principles, the family values I cherish. People talk and what if they do. It is none of my business what they think of me, of us, of this wounded relationship. Poets do not know how to live. We only know how to die.

Sylvia and Ted

'Ha, whatever happened to the mutual admiration club when I adored the poet Ted Hughes?'

'You sometimes astonish me. I think that everyone in the universe is not without a fair amount of damage and surely you can see that I'm not.'

'It is just that they go undercover with it. You have decided that is not you and that is not the way forward for you.

'I love you.'

'Is that supposed to mean something to me?'

'We took vows.'

'Now you're going to bring God into this.'

'You're attacking the wrong person, Sylvia. I haven't committed any wrong.'

Journal entry

Daily I get glimpses of the portrait of a writer. It feels kind of surreal to me (more like a dream) especially the consciousness of the writer and the 'thought-magic' that we wield and that we harbour in our communities. In front of the writer lies a battlefield. The portrait's skin and its flesh and bone and blood are made up of history and poverty, the divide between everything that came before, the divide that lies between the powerful and the vulnerable and a rich diversity. It houses the thought and the community I have spoken of before. At heart we, the writer are creative beings. The poet is the mystic being finding everything around him bearable and unbearable. Always reckoning those two forces of nature, those two cycles, seasons in the circle of life. I write because it's my life. Writers write because it is their saving grace. I write because I don't know what to do with the raw energy I have of blood and guts.

Sylvia and Ted

'I haven't committed adultery.'

'You don't know the meaning of the words humanity and right, Ted. I have the right to live my own life. The same way you do now. You feel you don't have to answer to anyone even a wife. And once our life together was a beautiful dream and now it's ghastly and miserable. We've failed at this. No, I've failed. There I've finally said it.'

'Listen to me.'

'Don't you, you, you fool get it? I don't want to listen to you. I don't want you. I don't need you. I don't crave you. You're not my emotional addiction. You're not my responsibility.'

'I am your husband.'

'Then why don't you start acting like one. A good husband, a good man for change or is it beyond your understanding and comprehension. Is it beneath you?'

Journal entry

I regard the world as delicious images crowding my mind, jostling for position and a fairy tale filled with angels and demons. There's always entrapment by ghosts. Oh, how they want to belong, those kindred spirits and what they wouldn't give to feel alive again. They vanish and appear at will and call our name in the wee hours of the morning scaring us half to death, they taste like air, smoke, honey, blood and they thirst for land. What they wouldn't give to walk and talk, speak truths and be tourists?

Today has been the colour of rain. A pale, washed-out colour and a dreary mood were hanging in the air but then Frieda smiled at me and then everything was alright in the world again. I am like a wounded animal, a hungry bear in the wild and there are days when I feel as if I am a woman on a mission. A mission to find love and I can't rest until I have rekindled it in the ones I have lost. Poetry is my voice, my light, my sport.

Sylvia and Ted

'If you like you can stop pleasing yourself. You can stop acting as if you cared what is happening to me. As if someone like arrogant you could actually give a damn.'

'You're pinning me in a corner.'

'Life is leaving the math and art and the creative spirit up to God. I have to look after my children and myself now.'

'Our children. They're ours, Sylvia. We created them together. They were not conceived via the Immaculate Conception.'

'You're getting mean now. Am I finally testing your patience?'

'I haven't left. I'm still here and that must mean something to you.'

'Mr Hughes, you're a caveman. You've burned me up. I have to save myself from you with serious intent before all my strength leaves me.'

Journal entry

I must be obedient and forgiving. Isn't that what a wife is supposed to be? He had the audacity to stand there and lecture me as if I was a bad person, a bad mother. Have I been a bad wife? I don't know. Have I neglected my children and been too self-absorbed? Perhaps, perhaps, perhaps. I don't find enough time in the day anymore to write like I used to. I remember how my husband used to help with little Frieda and especially Nicholas when I wanted some time to myself. But most importantly when I wanted to write. When I first met Ted all I wanted to do was make him happy. To see him smile, read his poetry and what an effort he made by reading mine and giving me helpful advice just lifted my spirits. It felt like a dream being near him, listening to him and now I have lost that dream and I must dream another. I have lost him to another woman. Is she better than I am? Is she a lady? Is she the perfect woman?

Sylvia and Ted

'The thing is Ted. In your quest for perfection, for this perfect life, perfect wife, perfect set-up of a family you forgot me. You forgot to take me along for the ride. Instead, you took your mistress because let's call a spade a spade, that is what she is.'

'I love you.'

'Once there was magic in your loving Ted but you've been telling tales. You've crossed the line.'

'I love you.'

'I'm not something to be possessed. You don't owe me anything. You don't own me.'

'They're my children and you're not taking them away from me.'

'You've lost and admit it. You just can't handle it. You can't handle me.'

'It's not a game, Sylvia. This is my life and my family you're talking about.'

Journal entry

I want to be a poet. I want to be a modern poet and I want to be the best modern poet out there. I just have to find a way out of this near-madness, this state of melancholy, the pathetic little me syndrome, the pain, and the sorrow that I feel comes upon me. I have to reach for the formidable and become that. I have to reach for the celestial. Depression is the sickness of our time. I see it all around me. In the sick, men who are stressed out by their jobs, women who have babies get depressed, people who leave home for brighter, greener pastures. Then there are those who retire, who get old, on the faces of immigrants and even the young people who go to university, people who get homesick for the loved ones they left behind. Ah, the pain of the mind the doctor would say to me. All you need is rest. You have a young family and they must keep you running up and down at all hours of the day. I've never stopped believing in that.

Sylvia and Ted

'I'm not going anywhere, Sylvia. I don't know what you have to forgive me for though.'

'Well, you should have thought about that before. You think you're blameless. You have wronged me. You have wronged Frieda and you have wronged Nicholas.'

'Don't bring our children into this.'

'Well, you should have thought about that before and don't raise your voice to me.'

'I wasn't raising my voice.'

'Then it was your tone. I don't like the tone of your voice. I said, you should have thought about that before you decided to cheat on me with that woman who will ever be anonymous to my children.'

'Where's your head, Sylvia? What are you thinking?'

Journal entry

Maybe it is all in my mind, the pain of the mind. I went to the doctor. I was feeling out of sorts. Not the way I usually felt and all he said was that the children and their energy must wear me out. So I was put into a situation where I had to agree. It is just this belief that I am something special because I have this talent. 'Don't gush. It's only poetry and most people find poetry obscure. Who reads it?' My mother said. 'Don't be in awe of yourself. Don't take yourself so seriously that you forget to see that God is in the details and all around you. Always remember that I love you for who you are. I don't think he is the right kind of man for you.' I have time now to reflect when I am on my own and he comes and watches the children for me and keeps an eye on them while I can get some work done. The writing of poetry does not come with instructions. Scientists dispel myths. Poets have to reckon with truth.

Sylvia and Ted

'You can hit me with a stick and beat me over the head with it but I promise you I won't feel a thing. I'm done with you. We're through, through.'

'I'm not treating you like a child, Sylvia but as unbearable as this situation is for you it is for me.'

'I'm unbearable when I'm sad. I'm unbearable when I'm moody or hungry or jealous of other women or your work that is your excuse for everything. You are a lost and little brutal man or boy, take your pick who has lost his toys or playing at cowboys and crooks with his toy gun or something. Why am I analysing you? I love seeing what I can do to you for a change. Nothing's going to get my suspicious mind down. Not you, not politics, not all the president's men and the queen's allies, not the British Empire and just not anything.'

Journal entry

There's something sensual about writing and the order and the routine in it. I wish it could last forever but it doesn't. It's temporary like the sun-age on the surface of a ripe cloudburst. I feel as if I'm an alcoholic, hippie or a druggie while I experience the sensation of the morning quiet. I take it all in. My consciousness becomes a dream factory that I am still trying to find all the answers to. It must be very cold where he is tonight, wherever he is. I don't care where he is and who he is with. If I did it might mean that I still love him, that I covet feeling the warmth of him beside me at night? He makes my heart and nerves still and soft. He fills my head with accusations and lies and every time that we come into contact now, I feel like a chip of glass. I must keep my chin up and my head held high but these days I'm prone to panic. What one earth will guide me to the courage I was once accustomed to having?

Sylvia and Ted

'You have lost me forever.'

'I'm not going to and have not taken you seriously when you are in this kind of mood.'

'Are you saying that between you and me, you are the world's best parent, best father? That's laughable.'

'Sylvia, don't go too far. You know that it's not good for you.'

'Father of the year is your ego still intact? Ever since I've known you, our married life together, everything has been as illusion.'

'What are you feeling? Despair? Are you angry? Speak to me. Tell me what's troubling you.'

'You won't understand. It's too deep. How on earth can you fathom disillusionment?'

Journal entry

When I enter the body of poetry a sense of fulfilment and satisfaction washes over me. There are explosions of tiny waves behind my eyes. My soul has made it thus far. I have to end the poverty in my mind but I find a cold comfort in the not knowing of things. If depression happened in nature what would we call it then? Would it be organic in origin? In a marriage when it ends whom is to blame for its demise. Who is the culprit? On the approaching betrayal in any relationship I have this to say. Lock down your heart dear and look away. It means that there may be something incomplete in the moving against the current of love. It means to love and die simultaneously. I think there's a theory behind light. When my body feels full of that stuff, the light, and the hidden energies in my aura I feel as if I have got free tickets to the centre of winter.

The Johannesburg People

I feel sick but I wait for this feeling to pass. It feels as if I wait for an eternity. It feels as if I have just licked the grimy asphalt beneath my heels. I'm trembling because I am cold. My hair is limp and straggly underneath my cap. My teeth long for a good bite. My teeth are tiny, shark teeth hungry for more. I haven't eaten anything the whole day. I am not hungry. I don't eat anymore. I pretend to push food around on my plate at night at suppertime and eat rice and peas (because they look beautiful, aesthetically pleasing on the plate). Why would I want to eat when every time I get high my appetite is sated? Everything becomes colourful, vivid, the cracks in the peeling ceiling and the seats, the thumbprint on the glass becomes sealed.

I am tired of the hierarchy of money, posse, model, celebrity, and hanger-on, poser, groupie, television executive and homosexual. They must all be valuable to society or otherwise they wouldn't be here tonight swaying their hips to the music, their lips and mouths are sensuous, drinking shots off the bar, spending money. Their identity remains a blur the entire evening but they are never quite out of your range, out of your peripheral vision with their entertaining quips and humour. Can I get you anything?

The girls are body beautiful but they are not much else I sniff. Pretty pictures, pretty paintings of expensive trendy fashion. Their clothes are tight, snug, figure-hugging – is there room for air? Their hair is freshly ewashed and blow-dried, their lips are wet, shiny, they are docile these sweet dolls, their movements are fragile and they will do anything for love. They will do anything for a guy they set their sights on tonight.

My head is filled with the glare of the glow of streetlights, cars buzzing dangerously low to the curb. I imagine the sidewalk will feel so cool as I rest my cheek against it.

I want to embrace the pavement, snuggle my head into the crook of my arm and close my eyes and sleep. I think I am going to be sick.

I am again reminded how self-indulgent the human condition can be. How we improve ourselves, our boring, safe, humdrum lives through self-medication through addiction, alcoholism, drugs, exercise and diet pills.

It is early morning. No one is around in the stillness of the darkness. There is only a vapour that descends on the deserted club, mist and ghosts. I have nowhere to go but down. So far down, that it is as far away from reality as possible.

I run in and out of the bathroom changing my top. I have one long-sleeved polo neck and one T-shirt. I feel sick and my face is flushed as if I have a fever. It is all pink and I shiver when I walk out into the darkness of the club, onto the dance floor. Two girls looked at me in a concerned way when I went in but they do not stop me and ask me if anything is wrong.

I want power. I go in search of it. I dance wildly because I am so happy, I do not care if I look like a total idiot. I speak to everyone because everyone is my friend. I forgive the world of all her sins. There are no evil people in this room tonight, only people who want to forget Hitler.

I am again reminded of how tough the human condition can be. People retching into toilet bowls into the early hours of the morning as the remnants of the party of the night before made itself known.

I have never felt more alone, more deeply unloved than I did that night. There are couples dancing around me, women dancing with women and men dancing with men, young girls with upturned faces kissing their

196

partners, making out. There were people sitting at the bar who spoke to me happily and I wanted to hold onto them and never let them go. I wanted them to stroke my hair and my face, the way my father used to do. They dance with me. They bought me drinks but they were not prepared to put up with me for longer than that evening. Was I not this perfect and invincible creature who could make people love her? Desperation clung to every pore in my body. I wanted to say, 'Can I come home with you? Will you be my family? What makes you happy? I promise I'll be good. I won't talk back.'

I went home but I didn't heal. I spoke to two therapists. One who was male and the other who was female.

I didn't fix my problems. The more I seemed to talk about them, the more solutions seemed to elude me, the more it seemed to me I didn't fix my problems, the more it seemed as if I was an accident waiting to happen.

I went home to look after my father and to realise what a mess I had become. I was such a mess that some people avoided me like the plague, even my brother and sister.

I like the city at this time of the night. There is no heat, only the air that rises up from the street, smoky and grey. The windows are lit like candles from the inside out like me only the light inside the buildings seems more stable.

Other women are the enemy. I do not have any female relationships. There were no female friendships, a female mentor, and a relationship with my mother or my sister in my life. I used to think it was because I wasn't beautiful like them. My shoes are starting to pinch my toes. I want to take them off and walk barefoot in this city I love so much because it hasn't chewed me up and spat me out yet. I wanted someone to take me in his arms tonight too and wrap them around me. Someone who would have told me it was okay to be afraid because he was scared too sometimes.

Instead I got stories, beautiful, intense, sad stories from people who were just like me, an invitation to a birthday man that I passed on. Their sadness was as intense as mine and for a short while they held me in the basement of the club. I felt safe as my world began to fall to pieces around me and I crashed and burned.

The sky is black and dark like a mesmerising black hole. There are no stars but I do not need stars. The sun will be up soon and already I feel the pressure of the upcoming workweek I have ahead of me. It is Sunday and I am going to church but there is a pit in my stomach. I was hoping by now it would be gone but it is still there, this smouldering pit. I do not smile. I do not laugh. Where am I going? What am I doing? I want to be loved. I am alone. I am tired of being alone, self-sufficient, independent and brave. My mind wanders through the service. I am thinking of my family and what they are doing but they call to find out how I'm doing.

I have a headache. It spills memories into the air that I do not want to think about but then I rediscover some of that happiness I experienced when I was growing up. It is very easy to feel unloved in the city. You are lonely. You do not have any contact with the outside world. Deep down, fiercely, you withdraw from all the loveliness in this world, in this city and walk with apparent ease, without any blame, your eyes have dark circles – bags under their eyes. I know later these morbid feelings of curiosity will disappear and I will regain my self-confidence but for now I am rendered speechless by the peaceful air.

I walk everywhere. I bite into the first taste of a muffin at a bakery in the morning. Crumbs fall into my lap. What happened this weekend almost could never have taken place in this sunlight? I feel content and blissfully happy. Nothing haunts me in the fresh air like it does when evening comes. The city has never looked brighter, cleaner but the colours lack their dewiness, their haziness of before. They have come into focus. My face is brighter. The images staring back at me, their lines are no longer blurred. I am not crashing down the street, veering, hurtling, careening wildly, lost into space. Johannesburg, you have never looked as beautiful to me now as you do today.

Genius behind the Closed Door

Ella's ghost sits at the foot of my bed staring at me with her long, sad, mournful face. I wait to hear for her footsteps in the dark. She keeps me company in the early hours. When dawn comes with the light filtering through the thin curtains, I turn around to look for her, but she is never there. Usually I am the talkative one and she listens. I mean with the state that she is in; all she can do is stare and wonder really what has brought the two of us together and who sanctioned 'it', this relationship. I am reading her books. I want to read all of them, push myself to get through it all, the real-life episodes, the real madness of her, her lovers, her experiences, the death of her son, separation from her daughter and the alcoholism but what I really want to ask her is, how do you love, how do you fall in love. Is it always an experiment? Does it always feel unnatural and disturbing when the person you're in love with leaves you, is someone always going to be hurt and the will the one on the receiving end of that hurt, that intense feeling of rejection and pain, relive it in recurring flashbacks?

I have many questions and I hope to find the answers to them in her books, the genius in her books. Ella, I want to say, help me. Help me to understand the cause and effect of the love affair (alone with all the difficulties of illness). What does that mean? To long for company, the smell of rain, to live and breathe solitude, birds singing, wind's song, sun disappearing behind clouds, cool breeze, father exercising and mother resting in the quiet of the afternoon, how I came to be in this world, alone, with my books and my writing, me with my sad, brown eyes and dark hair, brittle soul and serious nature. Now look at me. Look at how far I have come. Look at how far I still have to go, the obstacles and challenges of my youth are no longer facing me. Over time things will change. I will become more set in my ways. Discontent my middle name, peculiar, peculiar,

peculiar, even more so at 32, with my life hanging precariously in the balance, no ring on my finger.

Was it all worth it? The bullying mother, the bullies on the playground, the matron and the captain hissing under their breath to mop the floor at the Salvation Army, clear the tables, wash the dishes, pack the crates, unpack them, the perishables going into the storage room, the meat going into the fridge, living even then in a dream world. Imagination, the consolation prize, always under the illuminating spell of imagination, gripped by its fierce call and something was loosed in me. Johannesburg and Port Elizabeth, always two cities rising up to meet me head-on, a crash test dummy set on a collision course with nowhere else to go but to meet the world in a thin line with hope put aside. A dummy that knew the final outcome would be misery. I would wash the crates. Wash them out with a hose, dry them with a damp cloth and then stack them up against a wall outside. They would be filled later that day with food from Woolworths. Was I happy doing this? No, not really but in a way it comforted me.

I was around people and that had to count for something. Something in me expanded. I wasn't that solitary figure that stood out in assembly. A stick figure, all arms and legs, awkward, who could hardly speak, open her mouth, stand her ground. I was around people who were like me, estranged from family, homeless rejects that had a low opinion of themselves, no sense of self-worth, who wanted to give of themselves but didn't know how. Somehow being around people like that made me a kinder, more sincere version of myself. I spent nearly a year at the Salvation Army and before that a few months at a shelter. Looking back on those times, I can sense it must have been a very frightening time for me but it went by in a flash and now I have adventures, poignant and sad, funny and wise to write about. The people I have met have become like well-known characters in stories, liked, loved very much and hated. I feed on their loss, my suffering, and the world that I saw in their eyes that was launched into the space around them.

And then there was my world. Sometimes I soared and there were other days I didn't. Those were the days when I took liberties with my neurotic female sentiment. When I preferred to slide under the covers, addicted to the warmth and comfort. No addiction is kind, I tell Ella. Did she just move her head in agreement, in my direction? She, of course, I have figured this out now, is just here to guide me. I understand all I have to do is talk. Whispering will suffice. I don't have to be loud. What does it take to be a writer, to write? Her eyes seem to say, you'll soon figure that part out elegantly. There is no need for you to be so superstitious but then again, those are clearly my words, not hers. I move backwards in time. I move to childhood. 'Age before beauty,' snigger, snigger, sniggering behind my back and then I am on the steps, on the way to class, my cheeks burning. I am turning red but no one can see. I am safe for now because no one can see. Tonight they were fighting again.

Although they closed their bedroom door I could still hear them, father as docile as a pet and mother screaming. What they usually fought about was money. If my mother loved me, she didn't say it. But was it all worth it, one tragedy and one adventure, one unfortunate discovery of the cruel and dangerous world in my life after the other. Yes, yes and yes. Overwhelming loneliness. What does that mean? First, you succumb to it and then you must overcome. I take long walks up deserted streets, through crowds, the lunch rush in the financial hub of Johannesburg. I talk animatedly to Ella as if I must make up for lost time, for something that I must still gain. She does not smile. But tonight she has turned away from me as if she knows something that I do not know. This is a loneliness that I must bear, it is my burden. How can I refuse it, refuse kismet? I am a grown woman, not a child yet I still feel as if there is something of the child about me. When will that change? When will sensibility start creeping in, a feminist intuition?

I pick up her book, Ella's book, lying next to me on the bed, the bed my parents bought when they were newlyweds. Smile Please, an unfinished autobiography by Jean Rhys. I run away too when I'm scared, if I start something and I fail at it, I quit it. I've failed at so many things. I've failed my family; I've failed my sister, society and the laws of the universe. When I've been presented with chances and opportunities, I've missed them or once again failed to see them. Jean Rhys is Ella's 'name'. It is Ella's book or rather the ghost's story, the ghost's life history. It is enough that she doesn't say anything, not a word. She shines. She glides. I am happy that there is no laughter here. Children's laughter can be particularly cruel, hard to take, harder to displace. I have learnt that game in a treacherous way. There are no bottles stowed away in cupboards or under the kitchen sink. Now why would I want to go and do something useless and stupid like that? I hate the taste of cigarettes and that cutting smell in the air. I want to live before I die.

Let's talk about love. And how the sun and the days compensate for the lack of you. The massive collection of the links to the chains of my material inheritance to this earth, landscape after landscape, Petrified Forest after Petrified Forest, castle after castle. You were my cure, my open window, my door standing ajar, my glass ceiling, my chipped tooth, angel perfected in youth already. You navigated and uplifted me the day you became exceptional (as I move towards immortality). You're my inheritance and editor, my Christmas present, hollow Easter chocolate egg and rain, my half-suggestion and implication. Now I fear no criticism or pain. Childhood transformations have come and gone. They have taken reading bedtime stories with them, discrimination, girls in their school skirts, white summer blouses, panic and youth's illustration. Another current's gone global and a river soughs in soughs out in and out of the ocean sea (perhaps Pacific, perhaps Indian). It is locked into that infinite eight.

Now there is only time for growing older, little time for little else, for everything. Your footprint's gone digital and mine is sucked into a sandal. And for those who like prose. There is nothing diminutive about it. It dissolves, you can distil it, the language's flowers, the routes you traverse in your mind's eye and the messages are never dull, cruel perhaps, mystical even. And for the once upon a serious lover that you were, you who had eyes like bees and skin as pale as paper. The man whose wife I wanted to be in the meantime and the hereafter. The man who I wanted to carry me through illness, and from youth to womanhood (he who had no red heart only a bleeding one). Your breath is rust, your heart is rust while he is far (far and away). In retrospect now I realise he was no miracle. While he hurt me and I wept, (I could not see that that intention was always there) all I could see was the lake of my hurt while I plummeted like a comet. You are a magnificent fish. Your fins have a brilliant colour and feel like oil on my hands. A swimming pool cannot be renovated. Alas! I am still me. I flicker like the faces of angelic children in a choir.

And for those who like poetry.

I reckon Ella always had an unstable greatness within her. Aren't all the greats born that way? She is my rival. There is nothing motherly about me except perhaps my clothes, the way I wear my hair now and I move differently in the world. I move 'on my terms'. And what about celebrity? Celebrities want publicity and they will sell their soul for it but what does the poet want? Do they really want a peace of mind or just peace or just to observe it, their soul observing it? Celebrities do not want our kind of empathy. They do not want us to relate to them at all. What the poet wants is this (eternal grace in the gaze of a child, a lion's courage through the looking glass of this wonderland of earth.) What the poet craves sorely is empathy and for the world to be kind to those who endure hurt, and who have to survive woundedness.

Once I found your lines on the page inviting (every curve, hollow, every vertical, every horizontal was home, a Hallelujah, was publicity, entertainment, scrabble, Communion, a tongue). I needed poetry then. It distracted me. Common sense no longer spoke to me (well at least not the way you did). And peace is so subtle even now. The truly great ones do not want to walk the road of intuition; they do not want people to be infatuated with them, to recite their words back to them verbatim, and they certainly do not want to be treated like some kind of an angelic host. They do not like publicity. Instead they (the best) shy away from it, from all of the cameras, the questions, and the starry-eyed gazes and wear self-effacing masks numbing themselves and all of their associations. They keep their hearts pure and their minds pure. The true ones commit themselves to a country of purity. They write odes, sonnets. It is essential that they do this to their heart's content. It is essential that they do not scorn haiku. It is essential that they do not scorn poverty but I want to pick at all of it. All chatter matters. And hell is like a brick to the latest swarm-buzz-attack shaking news-day to the head.

And how did Ella come to find intelligence, tragedy-multiplied, anchored into life's sequences of despair, moving scenes, moving pictures, the roles men played in her life, the rogues, her rivals (of course other women and her sisters, aunts), and the scenarios of playing playful husbands and wives. Could she fathom wedding cake as she did prose?

Once I found her I always found imagination.

Regarding Helen

This is how I remember Helen Martins. The Magi and the Owl House; their tethers tug like a flame at my heartstrings and I wonder about her wounds, her coy magical healing, did she ever prepare a delicious, warm cake for her friend, that social worker that Fugard spoke so highly of. What stalked her for so long; a lifetime and then she had to go and die still so young, fighting fit? Oh, suicide is a forlorn, lonely way to go. Don't do it, I would have said and she would have looked at me. Our eyes, I imagined would have connected the way the white sunlight connects with the angles and corners of shadows of furniture, against the wall, against the panes, against panels and cupboards, on summertime afternoons and then I would have understood her motives, the intention behind it all, the mystery, the spell that 'it', suicide, had cast over her, her life's work and as I wander through her house I can feel her presence.

I don't think her unstable. She doesn't haunt me, my waking thoughts as much as her body of magnificent work, her 'art' does; if I can call it that. Writers write, poets lose themselves in translation, philosophers who pose as academics during the day intellectualise debate over wine and sushi until the early hours of the morning. When did she know her jig was up, that her time had come to bid this cruel world adieu in the worst possible way? Who found her with her insides eaten away? I read Fugard's The Road to Mecca. I was jealous. Jealousy and cowardice are in the sticky blood of every writer and it simply does not boil away to a faint, hot zone of grieving nothingness, fumbling bits and pieces like crushed autumn leaves dead in the centre of the flushed palm of your hand. Helen's Mecca cast its own spell on me. To me it felt magical. A love spell launched into the language of the pathways of a warring fraction of nerves, anxious to please like a child with the limbs, eyes, soft, sweet-smelling tufts of hair and a smile of a doll's features and yet, a spell that was blank up front, to take comfort in that blankness as if it was purified like a chalice of Communion wine and it was also a spell that spelt, 'be faithful as a servant of God, a man of the cloth'.

He, Fugard, seemed to craft the impossible in a way that did justice to Helen, the insecure, little, belittled bird afraid of the outside world; Helen, the Outsider in a way I knew I could never because I did not get the 'hook', the 'bait' but fishing for information, our keen sense, our powers of observation of human behaviour is what writers and poets know best as we drink our coffee, brew pots of tea, grow a hunched back bent over our ancient computer. How did she, Helen who was not so insecure after all, build that wall around her? How did she approach each subject, each project; as an assignment? Did she miss the feeling of the warmth in her bedroom of another human being? The company of her dead husband, their daily rituals filled with breakfasts, hot, buttered toasts, meals that came out of cans, processed foods that could easily be heated up and eaten with bread like pilchards or sardines. They would probably have imbibed hot drinks during the day; warm milk at bedtime, lukewarm tea when it was called for, the bitter taste of coffee with grounds at the bottom of the cup in the morning. I think she had an inkling she would live on even in death and in her gift that she left to the world, was the method in her madness.

Did these apparitions that came to life see her as a mystic; a prophetess bound for crucifixion and resurrection, with her own shroud of Turin, God forbid, did they come to life under her splayed fingertips, come to her from above, heaven-sent, as natural as night and day? Were they angelic utterances whispered in her ear while she slumbered, as she turned in her sleep, twisting the sheets between her legs until finally she dreamed until daybreak or were they the of hallucinations induced by the isolated

207

landscape, the barren countryside which surrounded her, the wilderness of her antisocial behaviour of her own making, induced by the mind of a woman slowly going mad, losing common sense, lacking that quintessential backbone of what made the English, the liberal-minded, so organised in their group or sporting activities like tennis for example, cricket or high tea; activities that required teams and cliques, so formal even in their games, proud of their progeny that followed in their footsteps, productive in the world, a world of their own making that was to a certain extent selfish, self-absorbed, not welcoming and friendly to people they considered to be not a fit partner in their climate; so genteel were they and conservative in their broad outlook on life. When I read of how people take their lives into their own hands I wonder what will happen, if there will ever be any substantial record of proof of their life here on earth. In the end, does it really matter to them, I question, yes, perhaps I judge their actions harshly and too quickly but to me it does matter because I was brought up that way; to believe that there is something holy and godlike about your spirit, your soul, your physical and emotional body and to take what does not belong wholeheartedly to you is stealing and there is nothing pretty about being caught after the act. If only, I imagine people who stumble across, infiltrate the place where the deceased lays, the body arranged in death, find the fragile creature as if taking a nap, resting, face composed, still, nothing amiss except the silence in the room where the unfortunate act of defiance, of quiet desperation had taken place without anyone's knowledge.

If only, I had come sooner, not said this, said that in a moment when all my thoughts were focussed perfectly, perhaps if I had acted swiftly but depression is both mean-spirited and long-suffering and there is no escape from that if it is passed down from generation to generation, inherent in the highly feminine woman prone to emotional outbursts, hysterics, tantrums, panic attacks, melancholy, mania, self-medication with painkillers and potions brewed with herbs and the effeminate man. Most people live in altered states of minds when something traumatic has happened to them. Most people think that therapy can help them with this. Sitting down face-to-face with someone who has studied the maladies of the mind for years and years they bear the deepest, darkest secrets of their soul and then leave, feeling relieved, as if they have just done something noble. They think they will find the answers their soul is seeking once a week ongoing sometimes for several years or for their natural life. They find someone who they feel is suitable, someone motherly, fatherly or someone young who reminds them of a loved one, someone they lost or who even reminds them of their own children or a substitute for the absent parent from their childhood and adolescence and young adult life. But I was really writing this about Helen Martins and for her, in defence of her and of the life she lived. Some people just can't help making waves and the more flawed they are, the more they can't stop making waves. Perhaps she found the answers she was looking for, the elegant solutions she craved as scientists or mathematicians craved in their own work, in her art, her sculptures, her friendship. I wanted to make sense of her thinking. What was it, inside her head that was making her tick insatiably, behind her eyes that was making her see, what exactly was her fruitful, the blooming flowers of her subconscious telling her to do, willing her to do consciously, conscientiously, consistently, efficiently and at a time unbeknownst to the world at large while she was still alive. In death, she has survived it all that she couldn't in life and yet she is still remembered as a woman made of skin and bone; a bone-woman, shapeless, caught in a thoroughfare like kittens to be drowned in a bag; her features like a sandscape, opening and shutting, through which seawater spills. Martyrs are made of this.

Mmap Nonfiction and Academic series

If you have enjoyed *Parks and Recreation* consider these other fine **Nonfiction and Academic books** from *Mwanaka Media and Publishing:*

Cultural Hybridity and Fixity by Andrew Nyongesa
Tintinnabulation of Literary Theory by Andrew Nyongesa
South Africa and United Nations Peacekeeping Offensive Operations by Antonio Garcia
A Case of Love and Hate by Chenjerai Mhondera
A Cat and Mouse Affair by Bruno Shora
The Scholarship Girl by Abigail George
The Gods Sleep Through It All by Wonder Guchu
PHENOMENOLOGY OF DECOLONIZING THE UNIVERSITY: *Essays in the Contemporary Thoughts of Afrikology by Zvikomborero Kapuya*
Africanization and Americanization Anthology Volume 1, Searching for Interracial, Interstitial, Intersectional and Interstates Meeting Spaces, Africa Vs North America by Tendai R Mwanaka
Africa, UK and Ireland: Writing Politics and Knowledge Production Vol 1 by Tendai R Mwanaka
Writing Language, Culture and Development, Africa Vs Asia Vol 1 by Tendai R Mwanaka, Wanjohi wa Makokha and Upal Deb
Zimbolicious: An Anthology of Zimbabwean Literature and Arts, Vol 3 by Tendai Mwanaka
Drawing Without Licence by Tendai R Mwanaka
Writing Grandmothers/ Escribiendo sobre nuestras raíces: Africa Vs Latin America Vol 2 by Tendai R Mwanaka and Felix Rodriguez
Nationalism: (Mis)Understanding Donald Trump's Capitalism, Racism, Global Politics, International Trade and Media Wars, Africa Vs North America Vol 2 by Tendai R Mwanaka
It Is Not About Me: Diaries 2010-2011 by Tendai Rinos Mwanaka

Chitungwiza Mushamukuru: An Anthology from Zimbabwe's Biggest Ghetto Town by Tendai Rinos Mwanaka

Soon to be released

INFLUENCE OF CLIMATE VARIABILITY ON THE PREVALENCE OF DENGUE FEVER IN MANDERA COUNTY, KENYA by NDIWA JOSEPH KIMTAI
Writing Robotics, Africa Vs Asia, Vol 2 by Tendai Rinos Mwanaka
The Day and the Dweller: A Study of the Emerald Tablets by Jonathan Thompson

https://facebook.com/MwanakaMediaAndPublishing/